Web Developer Foundations

Introduction to Dreamweaver MX

Terry A. Felke

D1122436

Web Developer Foundations: Introduction to Dreamweaver MX
Terry Felke
William Rainey Harper College

ZYX 432
ISBN: 1-57676-135-5

The publisher wishes to acknowledge the memory and influence of James F. Leisy. Thanks, Jim. We miss you.

Text and Cover Design: Mario Rodriguez
Copyediting: Carol Noble
Composition: Joshua Faigen
Proofreading: Kristin Furino, Holbrook Communications
Book Manufacturing: Corley Printing Company

Scott/Jones Publishing Company
Editorial Group: Richard Jones, Mike Needham, Denise Simon, Leata Holloway, and Patricia Miyaki
Production Management: Audrey Anderson
Marketing and Sales: Victoria Judy, Page Mead, Hazel Dunlap, Hester Winn and Donna Cross
Business Operations: Michelle Robelet, Cathy Glenn, Natascha Hoffmeyer and Bill Overfelt

A Word About Trademarks

All product names identified in this book are trademarks or registered trademarks of their respective companies. We have used the names in an editorial fashion only, and to the benefit of the trademark owner, with no intention of infringing the trademark.

.NET, ASP, ASP.NET, FrontPage, FrontPage Server Extensions, Internet Explorer, Microsoft, MS, Windows, Windows Explorer, and Word are trademarks of Microsoft Corporation.

Adobe and PhotoShop are trademarks of Adobe Systems Corporation.

JavaScript and JSP are trademarks of Sun Corporation.

ColdFusion, ColdFusion MX, Dreamweaver, Dreamweaver MX, Fireworks, Fireworks MX, Flash, Flash MX, and Flash Player are trademarks of Macromedia Corporation.

Netscape and Netscape Navigator are trademarks of Netscape Communications Corporation.

Additional Titles of Interest from Scott/Jones

Computing with Java™: Programs, Objects, Graphics,
    Second Edition and Second Alternate Edition

From Objects to Components with the Java™ Platform
Advanced Java(tm) Internet Applications, Second Edition
    by Art Gittleman

Developing Web Applications with Active Server Pages
    by Thom Luce

Starting Out with Visual Basic
Standard Version of Starting Out with C++, Third Edition
Brief Version of Starting Out with C++, Third Edition
    by Tony Gaddis

Starting Out with C++, Third Alternate Edition
    by Tony Gaddis, Judy Walters, and Godfrey Muganda

C by Discovery, Third Edition
    by L.S. and Dusty Foster

Assembly Language for the IBM PC Family, Third Edition
    by William Jones

QuickStart to JavaScript
QuickStart to DOS for Windows 9X
    by Forest Lin

Advanced Visual Basic.Net, Third Edition
    by Kip Irvine

HTML for Web Developers
Server-Side Programming for Web Developers
    by John Avila

The Complete A+ Guide to PC Repair

The Complete Computer Repair Textbook, Third Edition
    by Cheryl Schmidt

Windows 2000 Professional Step-by-Step
Windows XP Professional Step-by-Step
    by Leslie Hardin and Deborah Tice

The Windows 2000 Professional Textbook
The Visual Basic 6 Coursebook, Fourth Edition
Prelude to Programming: Concepts and Design
The Windows XP Textbook
    by Stewart Venit

The Windows 2000 Server Lab Manual
    by Gerard Morris

Preface

Web Developer Foundations: Introduction to Dreamweaver MX is intended for use in a first semester web development course. The purpose of the booklet is to introduce Macromedia Dreamweaver MX and give students practice with the following skills:

- Creating a Dreamweaver site
- Creating a web page
- Adding content to a web page
- Setting page properties
- Adding images to a web page
- Creating hyperlinks and e-mail links
- Adding tables to a web page
- Designing a page with a tracing image
- Using layout view
- Creating Flash text and Flash buttons
- Applying Dreamweaver validation and accessibility testing
- Publishing a Dreamweaver site

A companion web site is located at http://www.webdevfoundations.net and contains additional material.

Organization

This booklet contains three tutorials that introduce Macromedia Dreamweaver MX. Tutorial 1 contains an overview of the application and walks the student through creating a simple web site. Tutorial 2 builds on the skills gained in Tutorial 1 as the students create a web site containing several pages, hyperlinks, and tables. The focus in Tutorial 3 is on special features of Macromedia Dreamweaver, including designing a page with a tracing image, using layout view, creating Flash text, creating Flash buttons, applying validation and accessibility testing, and publishing. The tutorials should be completed in order.

Features of the Booklet

- **Hands-On Practice.** These tutorials are meant to be read while the student is at a computer. The student is encouraged to work along with the booklet.
- **FAQ.** The author has taught web development courses for several years and is frequently asked similar questions by students. These have been included in the book and are marked with a special FAQ logo.

- **Student Supplements.** A student disk is included with each book that contains the images used in the tutorials.

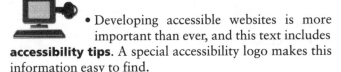 - Developing accessible websites is more important than ever, and this text includes **accessibility tips**. A special accessibility logo makes this information easy to find.

- **Instructor Supplements.** The Web Developer Foundations: Using XHTML Instructor Materials CD contains tutorial solutions. A special instructor area on the companion web site at http://www.webdevfoundations.net contains additional syllabi and a resource area for all Instructors using this text. Contact your publisher's representative for the Instructor Materials CD and for the password for instructor area on the course web site.

Acknowledgements

There are many people who contributed to this booklet. I'd like to thank Richard Jones, Denise Simon, and Audrey Anderson at Scott/Jones Publishing.

Thanks are in order to the adjunct faculty members at William Rainey Harper College who student-tested the first version of these tutorials; most notably Savarra Anderson, Geetha Murthy, and Jasmina Panikov. I would also like to thank my husband, Greg Morris, for his patience, understanding, support, and encouragement.

About the Author

Terry Felke is an Assistant Professor at William Rainey Harper College in Palatine, Illinois. She holds a Master of Science degree in Information Systems and various certifications, including Microsoft Certified Professional, Master CIW Designer, and CIW Certified Instructor.

Ms. Felke published her first web site in 1996 and has been working with the Web ever since. She helped to develop the Web Development Certificate and Degree programs at Harper College and currently is the lead faculty member in that area.

Table of Contents

Introduction

Some consider Macromedia Dreamweaver to be the most popular authoring tool used by professional web developers. Macromedia recently stated that there are over 700,000 registered Dreamweaver users. You will explore this popular application in this text.

Dreamweaver MX Tutorial 1

Dreamweaver MX is used to create and publish web sites. The Dreamweaver development environment is comprised of a number of menus, windows, and panels. In Dreamweaver MX, these are grouped together in the Dreamweaver workspace.

Dreamweaver offers some handy productivity features, including the ability to edit the HTML and the web page document side by side access to reference material; automatic generation of JavaScript for commonly used interactivity easy generation of Flash text and Flash buttons, and publishing using built-in FTP.

Dreamweaver can be used to keep track of web page files and even automatically change links when you rename or move files within your Dreamweaver web site, called a Dreamweaver site. Dreamweaver MX does not offer built-in server-side processing like Microsoft FrontPage does with the FrontPage Server Extensions. However, Dreamweaver MX adds new support for building ColdFusion MX, ASP.NET, and PHP web sites and increased support for development of ASP, JSP, and legacy ColdFusion applications. These are beyond the scope of this text, but provide features that experienced web developers find helpful. A web site created with Dreamweaver can be published to any web server—there are no special server extensions needed, as with FrontPage.

In this tutorial, you will begin to become familiar with the graphical user interface of Dreamweaver and create your first Dreamweaver site.

The Dreamweaver Workspace

The Dreamweaver workspace is shown in Figure 1. It contains many components designed to improve your productivity including a tabbed Insert bar, the document window, dockable panel groups on the right-hand side, and customizable toolbars. This section will examine some commonly used components.

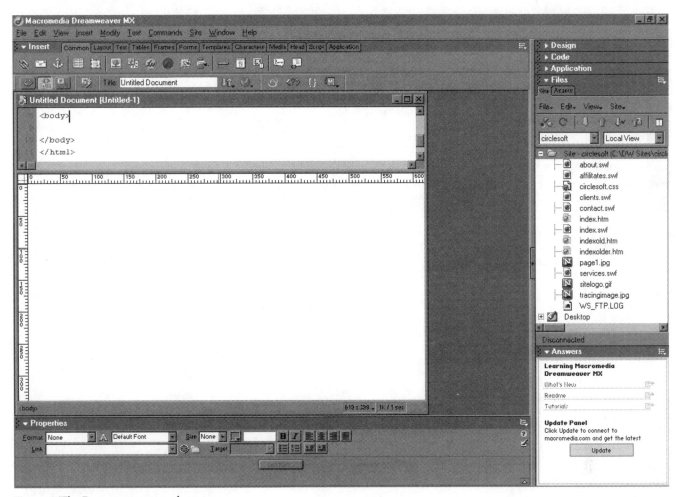

Figure 1 *The Dreamweaver workspace*

The Document Window

The Document window is where you edit web pages. Figure 2 shows the Document window that is part of the Dreamweaver workspace. The Document window can show both the Code view and the Design view at the same time. This allows web developers to move back and forth between coding and designing quite easily.

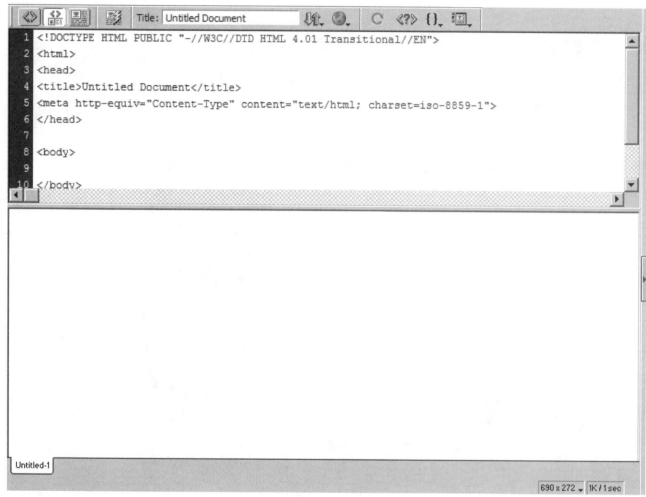

Figure 2 *The Document window*

As you view Figure 2 notice that the top half of the Document window displays the Code view. The code created by Dreamweaver when it is first installed is HTML, not XHTML. One of the advantages of Dreamweaver is the ease of customization. You will learn to configure Dreamweaver to create XHTML later in this tutorial. The lower half of the Document window displays the Design view, which is a WYSIWYG (what you see is what you get) editor.

The bottom panel of the Document window, shown in Figure 3 contains some useful features.

Figure 3 *The bottom panel of the Document window*

The Tag Selector is on the left side. It displays the HTML tags associated with a selected element. In Figure 3 a body tag has been selected.

The Window Size pop-up menu displays the measurement in pixels of the document window. It includes a drop-down arrow that can be used to quickly change the size of the Document window. See Figure 4 for a detailed view. This feature could be helpful you are when designing for various screen resolutions.

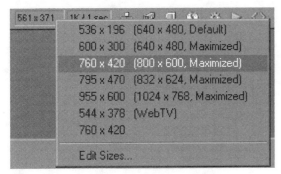

Figure 4 *Configuring the window size*

The Document Size / Download indicator, on the far right, displays the current size of the document and the length of download time at 28.8Kbps.

The Document Toolbar

The Document toolbar, shown in Figure 5, is located above the Document window in the Dreamweaver workspace. It contains buttons and pop-up menus that provide different views of the Document window (such as Design view and Code view), a text box to configure the page title, and some operations, such as previewing in a browser.

Figure 5 *The Document toolbar*

The Document toolbar contains a number of buttons. You can place the mouse pointer over a button for a description of its purpose. The three buttons on the left control the view shown in the document window.

The Code View button shown in Figure 6 (F10 is the shortcut key), changes the display in the Document window to all code.

Figure 6 *Code View button*

The Split Screen View button shown in Figure 7, displays both Code view and Design view in the Document window.

Figure 7 *Split Screen View button*

Figure 8 shows the Design View button. This changes the display in the Document window to the Design view.

Figure 8 *Design View button*

The Title text box (shown in Figure 5) provides a convenient spot to modify the document title. Other Buttons that are useful on the Document toolbar are the Preview/Debug in Browser button (Figure 9),

Figure 9 *Preview/Debug in browser button*

the Reference button (Figure 10),

Figure 10 *Reference button*

and the View Options button (Figure 11).

Figure 11 *View Options button*

The Preview/Debug Button allows you to configure and select the browsers you plan to use to test your web pages. F12 is the shortcut key to preview a web page in a browser when you use Dreamweaver. The Reference button provides access to the O'Reilly HTML, JavaScript, and CSS documentation in the Reference panel (see Figure 12). The View Options button configures features including word wrap, line numbers, and rulers in the Document window.

The Menu Bar

Figure 13 *The Menu bar*

The Menu bar, shown in Figure 13, controls functions such as saving files, copying, inserting images, modifying tables, formatting text, selecting commands, configuring the site, and displaying various windows. Dreamweaver Help, also accessed from the Menu bar, contains help files that are searchable, and includes a "What's New" presentation and tutorials to get you started with the application.

The Insert Bar

The Insert bar, shown in Figure 14, contains buttons for inserting components such as links, images, tables, and forms into a document. The Insert bar is new to Dreamweaver MX and includes the functions of the Object palette that was used in earlier versions of Dreamweaver. If the Insert bar is not visible in your Dreamweaver workspace, select Window, Insert from the Menu bar.

Did you say documentation?

Yes, Dreamweaver is bundled with a number of online reference manuals. The online references are context-sensitive and searchable. A partial screen shot of the O'Reilly CSS Reference panel is shown in Figure 12. What handy material to have right at your fingertips!

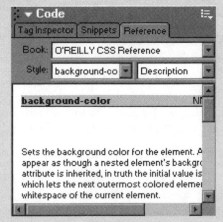

Figure 12 *The Reference panel can be found docked on the right side of the Dreamweaver workspace in the Code panel.*

Figure 14 *The Insert bar is a tabbed interface with many options.*

As shown in Figure 14, the Insert bar is a tabbed interface. The tabs are categories of objects that can be used on a web page: Common, Layout, Text, Tables, Frames, Forms, Templates, Characters, Media, Head, Script, and Application. Each tab contains a number of buttons. To determine the function of a button, place the mouse pointer over the button and wait for a brief description to appear. In Figure 14, the mouse was placed over a button with a picture. The description indicates that this is the Image button. The Image button is used to add an image to a web page.

This tutorial concentrates on the most commonly used features of the Insert bar. The Common tab, shown in Figure 14, is used to work with a number of components, including hyperlinks, e-mail links, named anchors, tables, layers, images, and Flash files. You will work with many of these components in the tutorials.

The Characters tab, shown in Figure 15, is used to add characters such as a nonbreaking space, quotes, and copyright symbols to a web page.

Figure 15 *The Characters tab on the Insert bar*

The Forms tab, shown in Figure 16, is used to create forms and form elements in a visual manner. You will use these and other panels as you complete the Dreamweaver tutorials.

Figure 16 *The Forms tab on the Insert bar*

The Property Inspector

As you work with Dreamweaver, you may find that this panel (see Figure 17) is most useful to you. The Property inspector is context-sensitive and dynamic. Select an object, XHTML element, or string of text and its properties will be displayed in the Property inspector. You can modify them and see the changes instantly in the Document window. In the example shown in Figure 18, the text "Hello World" was highlighted and the Property inspector was used to choose Arial font, size 4, and italic.

Figure 17 *The Property inspector*

Notice also the Tag Selector in Figure 18—as options were set in the Property inspector, Dreamweaver added the **<font>** and **<em>** XHTML tags to the document. These tags were then displayed in the Tag Selector.

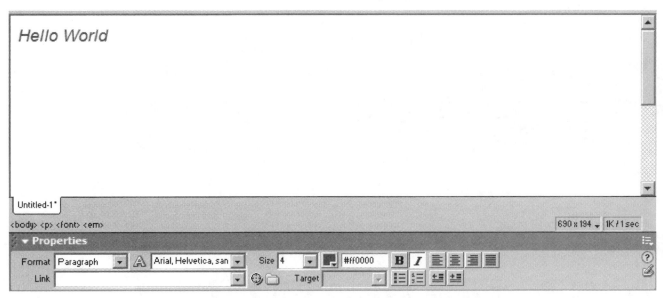

Figure 18 *The Document window Design view, Tag Selector, and Property inspector*

Some elements, such as images, have a large number of properties. The most commonly used properties are always displayed. There is a small trianglular button, shown in Figure 19, in the lower right-hand corner of the Property inspector; click on this when you need to access additional properties.

Figure 19 *Click on this button to display additional properties in the Property inspector.*

If the Property inspector is not visible in your Dreamweaver Environment, select Window, Properties from the Menu bar. See Figure 20.

Figure 20 *Use the Window option on the Menu bar to display any windows, panels, and palettes.*

The Panel Groups

The panel groups are located on the right-hand side of the Dreamweaver workspace and provide additional functions under the categories of Design, Code, Application, Files, and Answers.

Figure 21 shows the panel groups in their closed position. Notice the expander arrow at the left-hand side of each panel. To expand a panel, click this arrow. The Design, Code, and Files Panels have been expanded in Figure 22.

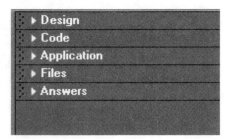

Figure 21 *The Panel Groups*

The Design panel is most often used to configure CSS and to add JavaScript behaviors to a web page. The Code panel offers a Tag Inspector panel that can be used to view tag attributes and values, a Snippets panel that can be used to add common code snippets to a web page, and a Reference panel that contains online manuals for technologies, including HTML, CSS, and JavaScript. The Files panel offers a Site panel and an Assets panel. The Site panel is used to organize and work with web site folders. The Assets panel can be used to visually manage components of a site, including images, multimedia files, colors, and scripts. The Application panel is helpful for experienced web developers as they build database-driven dynamic web applications with server-side programming or scripting. The tutorials in this booklet do not use the Application panel.

The Answers panel, shown in Figure 23, is useful for all web developers and offers direct links to the What's New presentation, tutorials, and a button to automatically get the latest Dreamweaver MX update from Macromedia.

Figure 23 *The Answers panel*

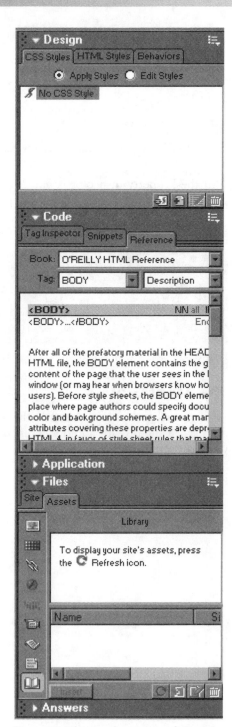

Figure 22 *The panel groups with Design, Code, and File panels expanded*

You have completed your whirlwind tour of the Dreamweaver workspace. This tour has touched on some of the commonly used windows, inspectors, and palettes. The next section explores using the Site panel to set up a Dreamweaver site.

Creating a New Dreamweaver Site

While you can edit web page files outside of a Dreamweaver site, some of the features (such as the Assets panel) do not function unless you are working within a Dreamweaver site.

Each time that Dreamweaver is launched it displays an empty Untitled Document in the Document window. If you do not need this document, click on the Close button (x) at the upper right corner of the Document window. Since you will be creating a Dreamweaver site in this tutorial, close the untitled document now.

Students often find that the process is easier if the folder that will contain the site exists before they create the site in Dreamweaver. Use Windows Explorer and create a folder on your floppy drive called hellodreamweaver. A screen shot is shown in Figure 24.

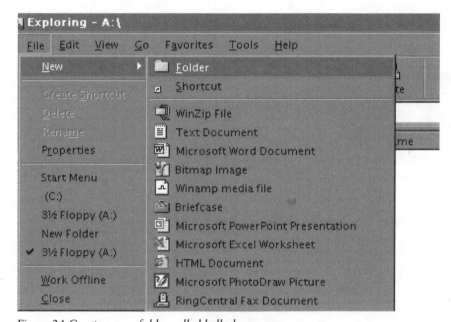

Figure 24 *Create a new folder called hellodreamweaver*

Defining the Dreamweaver Site

Once your folder exists, the next step is to use Dreamweaver to define the site. The Site panel, shown in Figure 25, is used to define and manage Dreamweaver sites. The Site panel is part of the File panel on the right-hand side of the Dreamweaver workspace. Using the Site panel, select Site, New Site to begin the process of defining a Dreamweaver site. See Figure 26 and Figure 27.

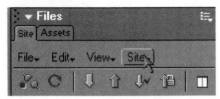

Figure25 *Select Site on the Site panel to work with a Dreamweaver site.*

Figure 26 *Select New Site on the pop-up menu to begin the process of creating a new Dreamweaver site.*

The Site Definition dialog box, shown in Figure 27, appears. Type HelloWorld for the name of your site. Click the Advanced tab.

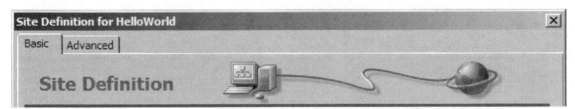

Figure 27 *Select the Advanced tab on the Site Definition dialog box.*

The Advanced Site Definition dialog box, shown in Figure 28, appears. This allows you to configure properties of your Dreamweaver site.

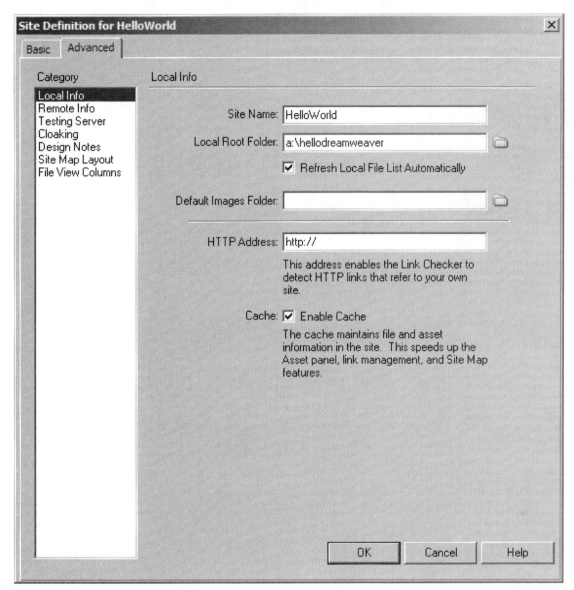

Figure 28 *The Site Definition dialog box*

Configure your local site to have a Site Name of "HelloWorld", be located on a floppy disk in a folder called hellodreamweaver. Leave the "Refresh Local File List Automatically" checked, do not enter a default Images Folder, do not enter an HTTP Address, and leave "Enable Cache" checked. The site cache keeps track of links and assets in your site so that Dreamweaver can quickly update them. Click OK and the Site panel will look similar to Figure 29.

Figure 29 *The Site panel for HelloWorld*

The Site panel provides a means to create, view, organize, and publish your site. It also provides quick access to the Windows desktop. The Site panel currently shows that your site has no pages. Your next step is to use the Site panel to add a page to your site.

Adding a Page to a Dreamweaver Site

There are a number of ways to perform most tasks using Dreamweaver, including adding a page to a site. In this part of the tutorial, we will use the Site panel to add a web page document to the Dreamweaver site that you just defined. Select File, New File in the Site window menu bar. See Figure 30.

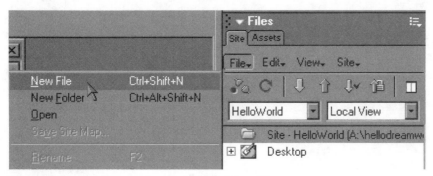

Figure 30 *Use the Site panel and select File, New File.*

The Site panel (see Figure 31) shows the new file as untitled.htm.

Figure 31 *The new file is added as untitled.htm.*

Rename the file index.htm as shown in Figure 32.

Figure 32 *The new file has been renamed index.htm.*

Double-click on index.htm to open it in the Document window as shown in Figure 33. Notice how the folder name and file name appear in the Title bar of the Document window.

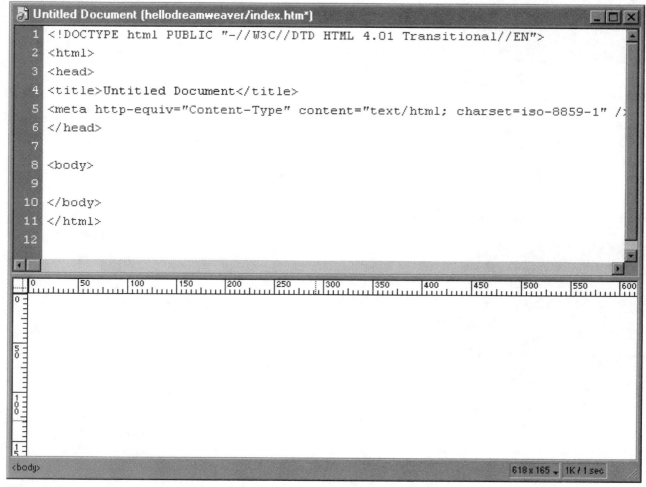

Figure 33 *The Document window now contains index.htm.*

Notice that the Code view shows HTML. Since XHTML is the most recent version of HTML, many web developers prefer to follow XHTML coding syntax. It is easy to configure Dreamweaver to use XHTML instead. Use the Menu bar and select File, Convert, XHTML as shown in Figure 34.

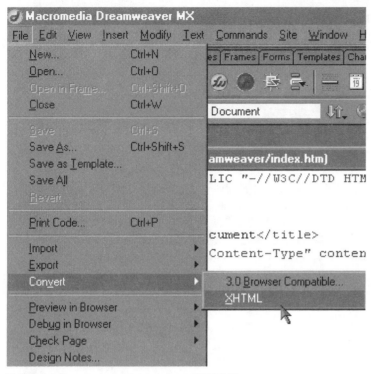

Figure 34 *Converting a document to XHTML*

Now the Code view should contain XHTML, as shown in Figure 35.

Figure 35 *The Code view now uses XHTML.*

Dreamweaver's preferences can be changed to always use XHTML. Use the Menu bar and select Edit, Preferences to display the Preferences dialog box. Select the New Document category as shown in Figure 36.

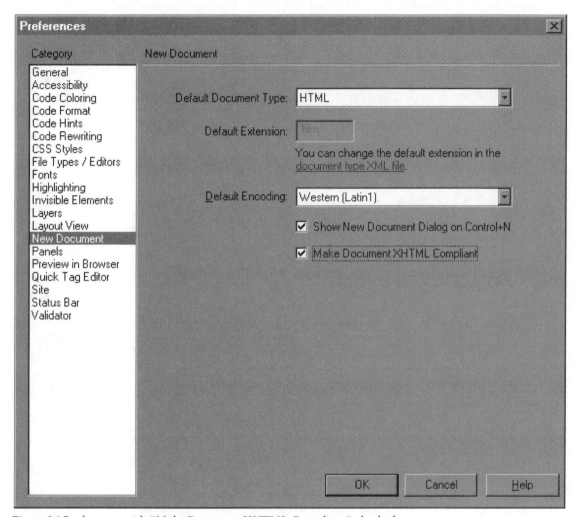

Figure 36 *Preferences with "Make Document XHTML Compliant" checked*

Leave the default document type as HTML but make sure that the "Make Document XHTML Compliant" check box is checked. Click OK. Now Dreamweaver will use XHTML for all new web page documents.

Now that the code is set to XHTML, you are ready to use the Dreamweaver workspace to edit the page. Let's start by adding a title to the page. A quick way to create or edit a page title is to type directly in the Title text box in the Document toolbar. Type in "Hello From (your last name here)". Next, click anywhere in the white space of the Document window and you should see the page title update in the text box and display in the Title bar of the Document window, as shown in Figure 37.

Figure 37 *Use the Title text box in the Document toolbar to modify page titles.*

Place your cursor in the Design view section of the Document window, type "Hello from Dreamweaver" and notice that the Code view is updated automatically. If you press the Enter key after your text, Dreamweaver will place paragraph tags around your message and create a new empty paragraph below it. See Figure 38.

Figure 38 *Dreamweaver writes the code right before your eyes.*

You have been working in the Split Screen view during this tutorial. The Split Screen view is one of the more powerful features of Dreamweaver—any change you make to either view (Code or Design) is immediately applied to the other. XHTML coders really like this feature because it allows them to know the effect of a tag immediately.

Remember that you can change the view using the Code view button (Figure 6) and Design view (Figure 8) on the Document toolbar.

Most of the code should be familiar to you. The page begins and ends with **\<html\>** tags, contains **\<head\>**, **\<title\>**, and **\<body\>** tags. Remember that Dreamweaver allows you to modify the code, even to change the syntax to XHTML. Let's concentrate on what Dreamweaver generated for you. The page title you configured was converted to XHTML code. Dreamweaver added a meta tag to identify the character set and encoding of the XHTML. As you create more complex web pages with Dreamweaver in later tutorials, you will notice other tags that Dreamweaver frequently adds.

You can feel free to modify the code if you need to. As you move your cursor in one view, it is moved in the other. Experiment by adding an exclamation point after the "Hello from Dreamweaver" text. Notice that the exclamation point is displayed in both views. Delete the exclamation point. You will have opportunities in later tutorials to work more with Dreamweaver's Split Screen.

Save the page by selecting File, Save. Test the page in a browser. Dreamweaver provides two shortcuts for this task:

- Press the F12 key.
- Click on the Preview/Debug in Browser button (Figure 9) on the Document toolbar.

Return to Dreamweaver and click on the Design view button (Figure 8) in the Document toolbar. In the next section you will explore the Page Properties dialog box and the Property inspector while you modify your page.

Exploring Page Properties

To access the Page Properties dialog box use the Menu bar and select Modify, Page Properties. See Figure 39.

Figure 39 *Selecting Page Properties*

The Page Properties dialog box that is shown in Figure 40 will appear.

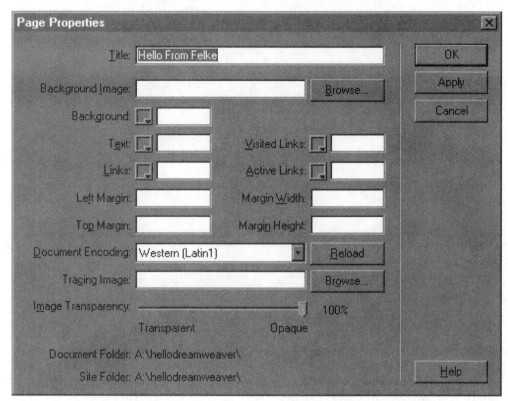

Figure 40 *Page Properties dialog box*

This is a convenient tool for applying properties to a web page such as title, background image, text and link colors, and margins.

Let's change the background color. If you have an exact hexadecimal color value, you can type it in directly in the text box. Many times you don't have a value or you need to match the color in part of an image or in another web page. This is when the color palette is convenient to use. Click on the drop-down box next to "Background" to display the color palette. When it first displays, the Color Palette shows an eyedropper tool that can be used to match color on another portion of the desktop. To use the eyedropper, move it to an area that is not on the color palette and click—your color value will be automatically entered in the background text box.

The Color Palette is displayed in Figure 41. Another method to choose a color is to place the cursor over a color box in the color palette and click—your color value is automatically entered in the background text box.

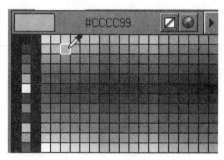

Figure 41 *The Color Palette*

Choose a light tan (#CCCC99) or another light color that is pleasing. Click OK to close the Page Properties dialog box. Your page should look similar to the one shown in Figure 42.

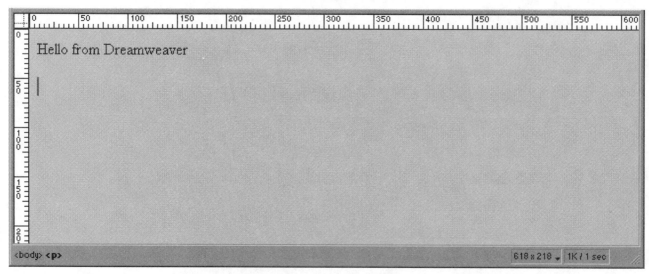

Figure 42 *The index.htm page with a background color*

By now you should be familiar with the Page Properties dialog box. Another method for displaying the Page Properties dialog box is to right-click anywhere in the Design view and select Page Properties from the pop-up menu. The next section continues your Dreamweaver tour as you explore the Property inspector.

Exploring the Property Inspector

Let's begin by using the Property inspector (Figure 43) to modify the text on the page.

Figure 43 *The Property inspector*

If the Property inspector is not currently displayed, select Window, Properties from the Menu bar.

Using the Design view document window, select your text "Hello from Dreamweaver" by highlighting it. Use the Property inspector to change the Format from "None" to "Heading 3" by using the drop-down list next to Format. Your page should look similar to Figure 44.

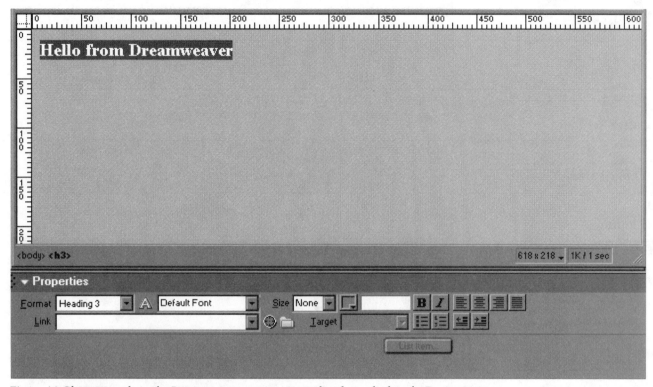

Figure 44 *Changes made in the Property inspector are immediately applied to the Design view.*

Now might be a good time to discuss the Undo feature of Dreamweaver. When you need to back out of a change, use the Menu bar and select Edit, Undo. Before you continue formatting the text, let's take a quick tour of the Property inspector.

As mentioned earlier, the Property inspector displays different properties depending on what object is selected. Figure 44 shows the Property inspector panel when text is selected. The parts of the Property inspector are listed in Table 1.

Table 1 *Property Inspector Components*

Component	Purpose
Format List Box	Configures the block level format. Select None (browser default), Paragraph (puts text in a paragraph), Heading 1 through Heading 6, or preformatted (places text between `<pre>` tags).
Font List Box	Configures a font for text display.
Size List Box	Configures the text size. Select None (browser default) or a numeric text size.
Text Color Palette	Arrow is used to visually select a color. Text box accepts typed in color value.
Bold Button	Toggles text to bold and back to normal.
Italics Button	Toggles text to italic and back to normal.
Alignment Buttons	Aligns text to the left, center, or right.
Dreamweaver Help Button	Launches Dreamweaver Help.

Hyperlink and Target Text Boxes

Configures hyperlinks and targets. You can type directly in the Link and Target boxes, click on the arrow to display a list of links (or targets) already used in the site, or display a file list by clicking on the folder icon.

Component	Purpose
Unordered List Button	Creates a bulleted (unordered) List
Ordered List Button	Creates a numbered (ordered) List
Text Outdent and Text Indent Buttons	Used to increase or decrease the indentation of text.
Quick Tag Editor	Invokes the Quick Tag Editor (Not used in this text.)

Now that you are familiar with the Property inspector, set the font to Arial, Helvetica, sans-serif (note how Dreamweaver automatically provides backup fonts in case your visitor does not have the primary font installed). Do not set the size for your heading. Click on the Color Palette icon to set the text color to a dark blue. Center the text with the center alignment button. Next, remove the highlight from the text by clicking anywhere else on the Document window. Your page should look similar to the sample in Figure 45. You will do further work with the Property inspector in later tutorials.

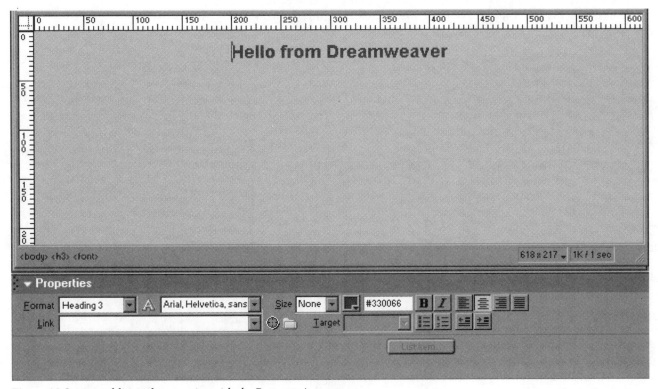

Figure 45 *Setting additional properties with the Property inspector*

Click on the Code view button to examine the XHTML that Dreamweaver created. Take a moment to examine it. When you are ready, save your page and test it in a browser. (Did you remember the F12 shortcut to preview your page?) This tutorial continues with an example of closing your web page document, exiting Dreamweaver, launching Dreamweaver, and accessing your Dreamweaver site.

Exiting Dreamweaver

To close a web page document, either use the Menu bar and select File, Close or click on the "x" button at the upper right corner of the Document window. To exit Dreamweaver, either use the Menu bar and select File, Exit or click on the Close (x) button at the upper right corner of the Dreamweaver workspace. When you launch Dreamweaver again, the most recent site you worked on will display in the Site panel. If you have not already done so, close the index.htm file and exit Dreamweaver.

Opening a Defined Site

If you defined your HelloWorld site on a floppy disk, place the floppy in the drive. Launch Dreamweaver and it will automatically display the Site panel with the defined site that you most recently worked with. Since you just worked with the HelloWorld site, it should display in the Site panel. Double-click on the index.htm file to open the page in the Document window. When you are finished, close the document and exit Dreamweaver.

If you work with multiple sites you need to know how to select a particular Dreamweaver site. As shown in Figure 46, use the Site panel, select the "Site" drop-down list to view the available sites, and select the site you need to work with.

Figure 46 *Using the Site panel to select a site*

Summary

By now you should be familiar with creating a site, modifying a web page, previewing the web page in a browser, closing the site, and reopening the site. A solid foundation in these skills will help you with other features of Dreamweaver. The next two Dreamweaver tutorials introduce topics such as adding pages and images, using lists and tables, creating hyperlinks, and adding Flash buttons.

You have completed Macromedia Dreamweaver Tutorial 1!

Dreamweaver MX Tutorial 2

In this tutorial you will create a sample site while you practice the following skills with Dreamweaver:

- Adding pages
- Formatting text
- Using lists and tables
- Inserting images
- Creating hyperlinks

The site is for a small vacation cabin rental company called MooseWood Cabins and has three pages: index.htm (Figure 48), cabins.htm (Figure 49), and reservations.htm (Figure 50). A site map is shown in Figure 47.

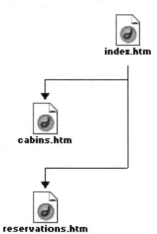

Figure 47 *MooseWood Cabins site map*

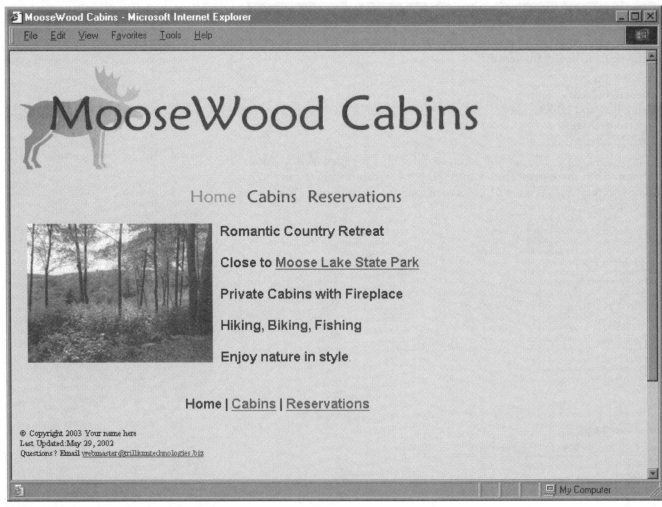

Figure 48 *MooseWood Cabins index.htm*

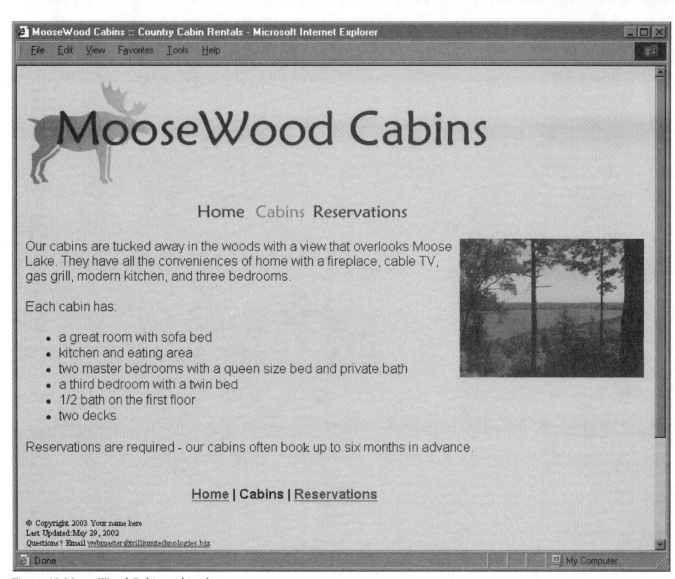

Figure 49 *MooseWood Cabins cabins.htm*

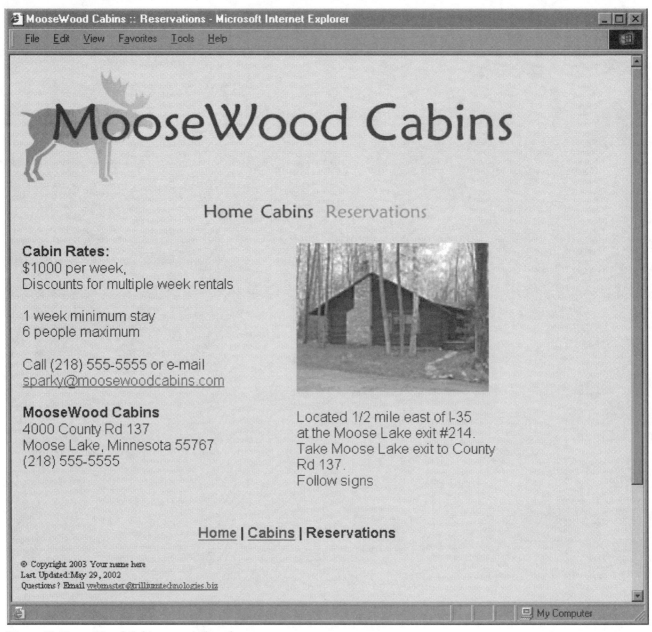

Figure 50 *MooseWood Cabins reservations.htm*

Creating a New Dreamweaver Site

Tutorial 1 introduced creating a new Dreamweaver site. This should be a review. Using Windows Explorer, create the folder for the moosewood site. Add a folder named moosewood to your floppy disk. Launch Dreamweaver and define a new site named moosewood that is located in a:\moosewood. (*Hint:* Use the Site panel and select Site, New Site.)

Adding a Page to a Site

After your site is defined, add a web page file to the moosewood site. One way to add a web page file to your site is to use the Site panel and select File, New File. A file named untitled.htm is placed on the Folder List. Rename the file index.htm. (*Hint:* Right-click on the file name and type in "index.htm".) This is the home page of your "moosewood" site. Double-click on the index.htm to open it in the Document window.

Using Images in Dreamweaver

Adding Images to a Site

The images used in this tutorial can be found on the student disk in the Tutorials folder. Copy the logo.gif (Figure 51), home.gif (Figure 52), home1.gif (Figure 53), cabins.gif (Figure 54), cabins1.gif (Figure 55), reservations.gif (Figure 56), reservations1.gif (Figure 57) moosewood.jpg (Figure 58), mooselake.jpg (Figure 59), and exterior.jpg (Figure 60) files and save them to your floppy drive in the a:\moosewood folder.

Figure 51 *logo.gif*

Home

Figure 52 *home.gif*

Cabins

Figure 55 *cabins1.gif*

Reservations

Figure 56 *reservations.gif*

Home

Figure 53 *home1.gif*

Cabins

Figure 54 *cabins.gif*

Reservations

Figure 57 *reservations1.gif*

Figure 58 *moosewood.jpg*

Figure 59 *mooselake.jpg*

Figure 60 *exterior.jpg*

Examine the Site panel for your moosewood site. The display should look similar to the sample in Figure 61. It shows the index.htm page and the images for your site.

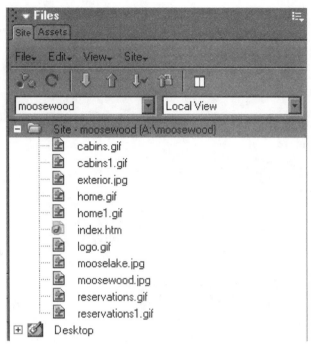

Figure 61 *The Site panel lists the index.htm file and the images.*

Wouldn't a quick visual preview of the images be nice? The Site panel and Assets panel are both in the Files panel. Display the Assets panel by clicking on its tab. Is your Assets panel blank? Click the Images button as shown in Figure 62.

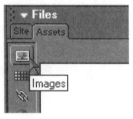

Figure 62 *Selecting to display images in the Assets panel*

Your images should now appear in the Assets panel as shown in Figure 63.

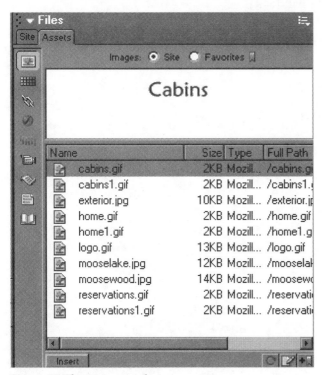

Figure 63 *The Assets panel*

Take a moment and click on each image name to display its thumbnail image in the Assets panel.

It's a good idea to organize your site by placing images and other media into their own folder. Create a new folder in your moosewood site called "media". You can use the Site panel for this task. Select File, New Folder as shown in Figure 64.

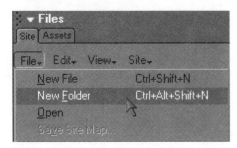

Figure 64 *Using the Site panel to create a new folder*

An untitled folder is added to the site. Rename the folder "media" and drag each image file to it. When you are done, your local Folder list will look similar to the example in Figure 65.

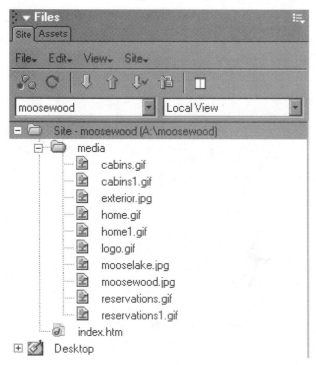

Figure 65 *All the images are now in the media folder.*

Now that you've got all the images for the site, let's start creating the pages for the Moosewood Cabins site.

Working with Images and Dreamweaver

Let's continue to work with Dreamweaver and build the home page of the Moosewood Cabins site. View the sample page in Figure 48 to see what you will be creating.

In previous steps, you created the moosewood site and added images into it. Your index.htm file may still be open in the Document window. If it is not, use the Site panel and double-click on the index.htm file to display it in the Document window. Now configure the page background color and page title. (This should be a review! *Hint:* Use the Menu bar and select Modify, Page Properties to display the Page Properties dialog box.) Choose a background color that is pleasing to you. Suggested colors include #E8E9CF, #FFFF99, or #CCCC99. The sample pages use #E8E9CF. Configure the page title to be "MooseWood Cabins".

Next, you will add the logo to the page. There are a number of ways to insert an image in Dreamweaver. Whichever method you choose, Dreamweaver writes the XHTML for you. The easiest way is to drag the image directly from the Assets panel. Display the Assets panel (F11 is the shortcut key) and drag the logo.gif file from the Assets panel to your Document window.

Another method is to use the Insert bar (see Figure 14) and select the Common tab. Click on the Image button to display the Select Image Source dialog box. Once the Select Image Source dialog box (shown in Figure 66) appears, select the media folder to display your image files. Highlight the logo.gif file and click OK.

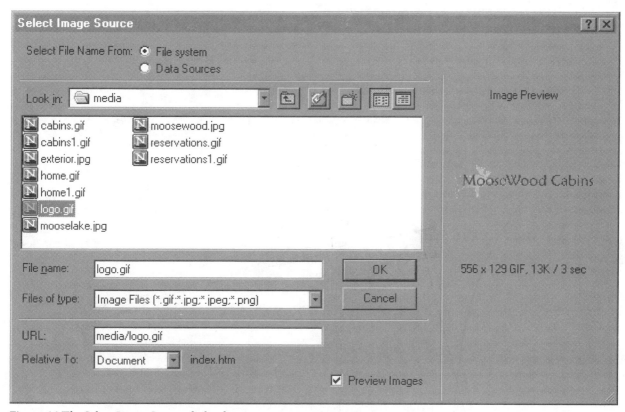

Figure 66 *The Select Image Source dialog box*

The logo should now be placed on your web page. Your home page should look similar to the sample in Figure 67. Save your page by selecting File, Save.

Figure 67 *MooseWood index.htm with background color and logo image*

Once an image is on your page you can move it and resize it if you like. You also can modify the image properties such as alignment and alternate text using the Property inspector. (*Hint:* Select Window, Properties or press Ctrl and F3 to display the Property inspector if it is not visible.)

 A sample Property inspector is shown in Figure 82.

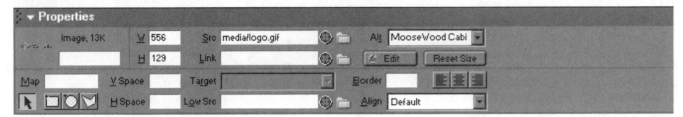

Figure 68 *The Property inspector can configure an image*

To configure alternate text for the image, type "MooseWood Cabins Logo" in the Alt text box.

Adding More Images to the Page

Refer to the sample index.htm page (Figure 48) and add the home1.gif, cabins.gif, and reservations.gif to the page. Be sure to configure each with appropriate alternate text. They will be used later as image links. Use the Text Indent icon to place them under the logo in a pleasing manner. Your page should now look similar to the sample in Figure 69.

Figure 69 *The index.htm page with additional images*

By now you should be comfortable with using Dreamweaver to add images to a web page. The next sections of the tutorial discuss text and image links, more text formatting, copyright symbols, and e-mail links.

Creating Hyperlinks with Dreamweaver

Let's continue to work on the home page of the MooseWood Cabins site and create the hyperlinks for the top navigation bar. Because this is the Home page, the home1.gif doesn't need a hyperlink. However, it would be great if the cabins.gif and the reservations.gif linked to their respective pages.

Click once on the cabins.gif to select it. If the Property inspector is not visible, display it either by selecting Windows, Properties or by pressing Ctrl and F3. Configure the hyperlink to the cabins.htm page. Using the Property inspector, type "cabins.htm" in the Link text box to create the hyperlink. See Figure 70. (*Note:* If Dreamweaver adds a border to your image hyperlink, use the Property inspector and set the border to 0.)

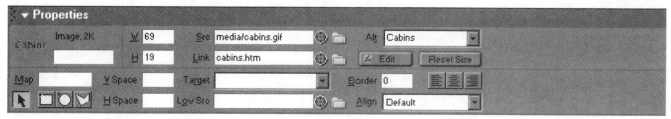

Figure 70 *Using the Property inspector to configure a hyperlink*

Another way to configure a hyperlink is to use the Menu bar. Click once on the reservations.gif to select it. Using the Menu bar, select Modify, Make Link to display the Select File dialog box shown in Figure 71. Type "reservations.htm" in the File name text box and click OK. Save your index.htm page.

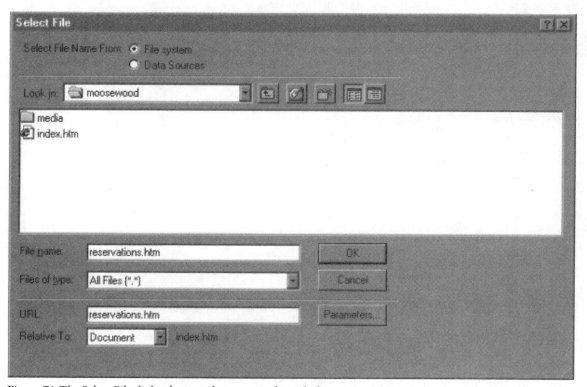

Figure 71 *The Select File dialog box used to create a hyperlink*

Text hyperlinks are created in a similar manner. You highlight the text that should hyperlink and either modify the Property inspector or select Modify, Make Link from the Menu bar. You will create text hyperlinks later in this tutorial as you add more content to the Home page.

Adding Content to the Home Page

As indicated on the sample Home page (Figure 48), you need to add an image of a wooded area and some text that describes the amenities of the cabins and surrounding vicinity. With index.htm displayed in the Document window, place your cursor on a new line under the navigation bar. Type the following text, pressing the Enter key after each line:

"Romantic Country Retreat
Close to Moose Lake State Park
Private Cabins with Fireplace
Hiking, Biking, Fishing
Enjoy nature in style."

Format the text using the Property inspector. Change the font to Arial and font style to bold. (This should be a review from Tutorial 1!) Your page should look similar to the sample in Figure 72.

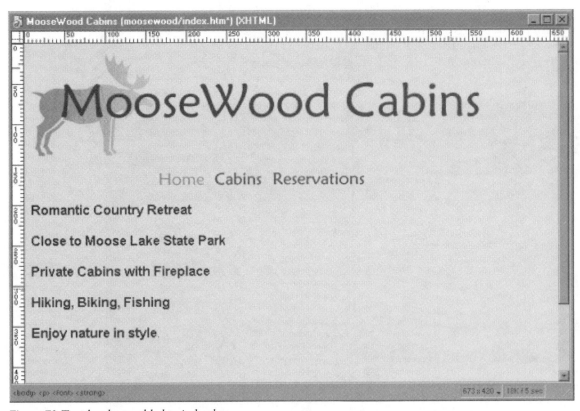

Figure 72 *Text has been added to index.htm.*

Add the moosewood.jpg image to the page and place it to the left of the *R* in "Romantic". (*Hint:* Drag the image from the Assets panel or use the Insert bar, Common tab, Image Button.) See the sample in Figure 73.

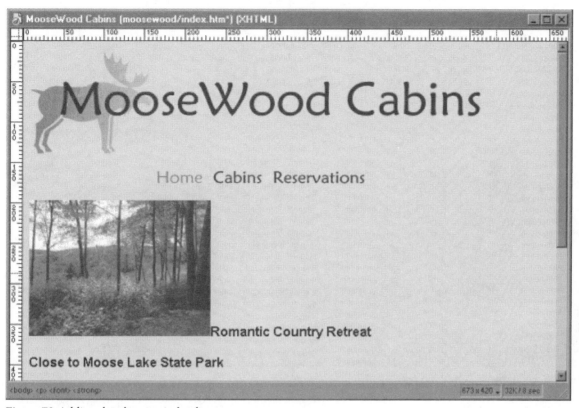

Figure 73 *Adding the photo to index.htm*

If you're thinking this isn't exactly like the sample, you're correct. There is still more to do. Use the Property inspector to configure the image to be left-aligned. Modify the Align list box to display "Left" as shown in Figure 75. Remember to configure alternate text. If the image seems to crowd the text, use the Property inspector and change the H Space (horizontal spacing) to 10.

Figure 74 *Setting the image alignment*

Your page should look similar to the sample in Figure 75.

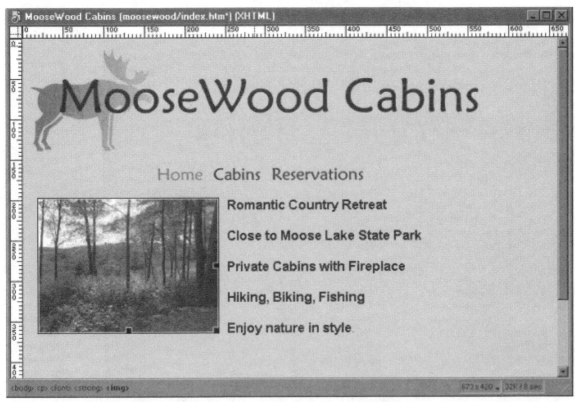

Figure 75 *The index.htm page after the photo has been aligned with the text.*

Now you are ready to create the text navigation bar for the home page (see Figure 48). Place the cursor on a new line under the content and type the following text:

"Home | Cabins | Reservations"

Use the Property inspector to format this text so that it is in the Arial font and bold. This text would look better if it were indented. Click the Text Indent button (Figure 27) on the Property inspector until you think the page is pleasing.

Now configure a text navigation bar by creating hyperlinks. Highlight the "Cabins" text and use the Property inspector to create a hyperlink to the cabins.htm page. Also configure a hyperlink from the "Reservations" text to the reservations.htm page.

As long as you are busy creating hyperlinks, take a look at the sentences you typed earlier in the page. The phrase "Moose Lake State Park" should link to http://www.wildernessinquiry.org/mnparks/parks/moose40.html. A sample of the page at this point is shown in Figure 76.

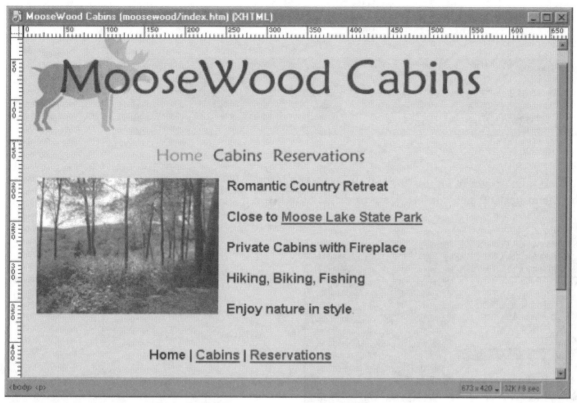

Figure 76 *The index.htm page with hyperlinks*

Adding Footer Text

The copyright, last date updated, and e-mail information should be added to the bottom, or footer, of the page.

Adding the Copyright Symbol

Place your cursor on a blank line under the text navigation bar. You might need to click the Text Outdent button (see Table 1) on the Property inspector a few times to place the cursor at the left margin.

Use the Insert Bar. Display the Characters tab and select the Copyright button as shown in Figure 77.

Figure 77 *Using the Characters tab on the Insert bar to add a copyright symbol*

After inserting the copyright symbol, type the year and your name. Press the Shift and Enter keys to move directly to the next line.

Adding the Date Last Updated

Type "Last Updated:" and configure Dreamweaver to automatically generate the date. Use the Insert bar, select the Common tab, and click on the Date button, as shown in Figure 78.

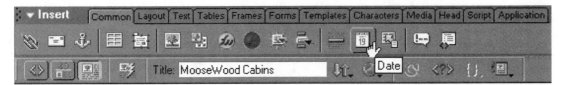

Figure 78 *Using the Common tab on the Insert bar to add a date*

The Insert Date dialog box, shown in Figure 79, will display. (*Note:* You could also use the Menu bar and select Insert, Date to display the Insert Date dialog box.)

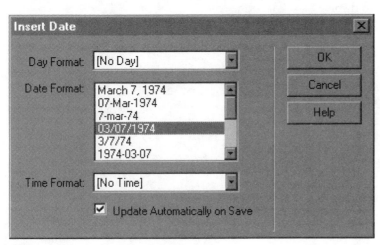

Figure 79 *The Insert Date dialog box*

Select the type of date format you prefer. Check the "Update Automatically on Save" and Dreamweaver will modify this date each time you update the file. Click OK.

Adding the E-mail Link

Now create the line that will contain the e-mail link. Press the Shift and Enter keys to move directly to the next line without leaving a blank line. Type "Questions? E-mail". Using the Insert bar, select the Common tab and click the Email Link button to display the Email Link dialog box (Figure 80). (*Note:* You could also use the Menu bar and select Insert, Email Link to display the Email Link dialog box.)

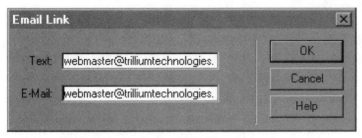

Figure 80 *The Email Link dialog box*

This dialog box allows you to configure both the text to display for the link and the actual e-mail address. Type "webmaster@trilliumtechnologies.biz" or your own e-mail address in both the Text and E-Mail text box values. Click OK.

Next, use the Property inspector to format the copyright, update, and e-mail lines to be Times New Roman font with font size value of 1. The bottom portion of your index.htm should be similar to the sample in Figure 81.

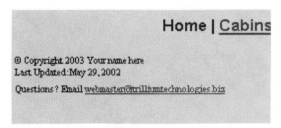

Figure 81 *Sample Page Footer*

Save your index.htm page. The tutorial continues as you create the cabins.htm and reservations.htm pages, and introduces lists and tables.

Adding Pages to the Dreamweaver Site

There are a few methods that can be used to add a page to a Dreamweaver site.

- In the Site panel (shortcut key F8), select File, New File.
- In the Site panel, right-click on the window, and select New File from the pop-up menu.
- In the Menu bar select File, New, select Basic Page, and click OK.

However, we are going to create new pages with many of the same characteristics as the Home page (index.htm). One way to be productive is to display the index.htm file in the Document window and then select File, Save As, and save the file with the name of one of the other pages. So—let's save a copy of the index.htm page with the file name of cabins.htm. Display the index.htm file in the Document window. Select File, Save As, type "cabins.htm" as the file name and click Save. See Figure 82.

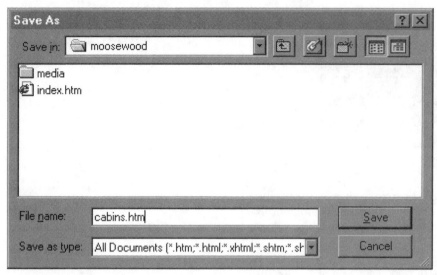

Figure 82 *Using the Save As dialog box*

The Document window now displays the cabins.htm page, as shown in Figure 83.

Figure 83 *MooseWood cabins.htm*

This is a great time to change the page title to a more descriptive phrase. Either modify the page title directly in the Document toolbar or use the Menu bar and select Modify, Properties. Change the tile to "MooseWood Cabins :: Country Cabin Rentals". Save the cabins.htm file. View the Site panel (see Figure 84) and notice that there is a new entry for cabins.htm.

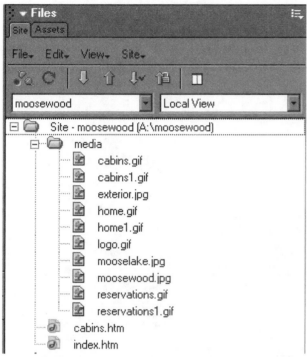

Figure 84 *The new cabins.htm file is listed in the Site panel.*

Adding Content to the Cabins Page

View the sample Cabins Page (Figure 49) to see what the page will look like. Notice the upper (logo and navigation) and lower (page footer) portions are similar to the home page. You will be changing the content—the middle portion of the page.

Delete the moosewood.jpg and the text from the middle part of the web page, leaving just the logo, graphic navigation bar, text navigation bar, and footer information. (*Hint:* To delete an image or text, select the item by highlighting it and then press the Delete key on the keyboard.) Place your cursor on a blank line under the graphic navigation and type the following text. Press the Enter key where indicated.

"Our cabins are tucked away in the woods with a view that overlooks Moose Lake. They have all the conveniences of home with a fireplace, cable TV, gas grill, modern kitchen, and three bedrooms. (Press Enter)

Each cabin has: (Press Enter)

a great room with sofa bed (Press Enter)

kitchen and eating area (Press Enter)

two master bedrooms with a queen size bed and private bath (Press Enter)

a third bedroom with a twin bed (Press Enter)

1/2 bath on the first floor (Press Enter)

two decks (Press Enter)

Reservations are required—our cabins often book up to six months in advance."

Format the text by changing the font to Arial. (This should be review! *Hint:* Use the Property inspector.) Your page should look similar to Figure 85.

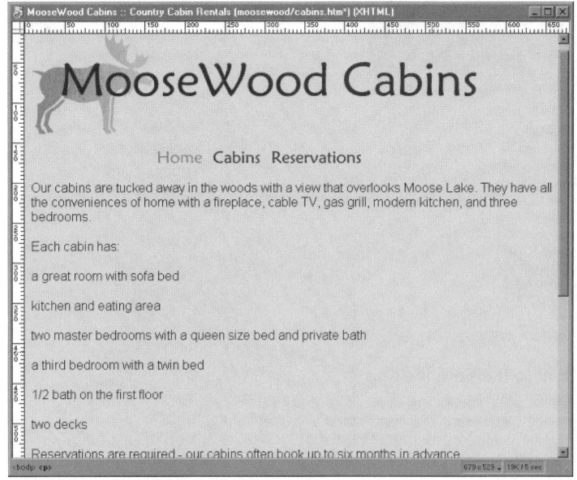

Figure 85 *Adding content to cabins.htm*

If you compare your page to the sample in Figure 49, you will notice that the phrases that describe the cabins should be in an unordered list. Highlight the phrases and select the Unordered List button on the Property inspector. If you had wanted to place the items in a numbered or ordered list, you would have selected the Ordered List button on the Property inspector. Your page should look similar to Figure 86.

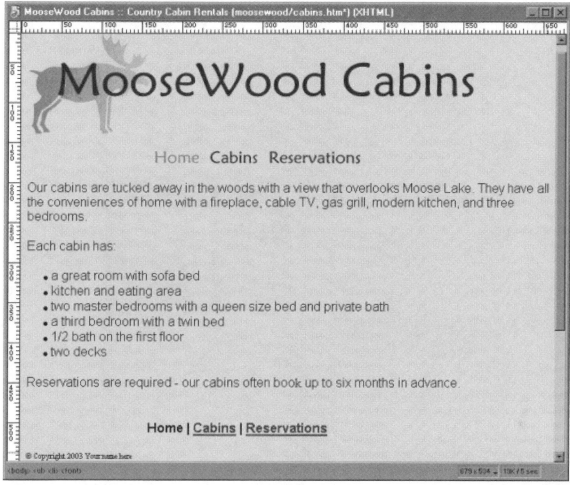

Figure 86 *The unordered list has been added to cabins.htm.*

Now add the mooselake.jpg image to the page. Drag the image to the page from the Assets panel and place it to the left of the O in "Our cabins". Use the Property inspector to configure the image to be right-aligned and to add an alternate text description for the image. Your page should look similar to Figure 87.

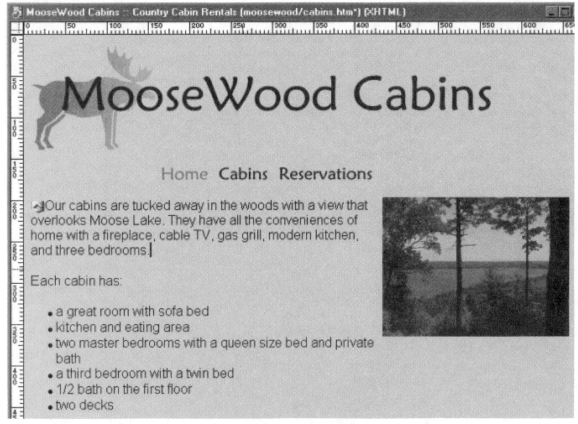

Figure 87 *The mooselake.jpg is right-aligned with the first paragraph of text.*

Notice that there is a gold icon where you originally placed the image. This icon will only show in Dreamweaver and will not display when the page is viewed in a browser. The icon indicates the placement of an object (in this case our mooselake.jpg image).

You can help web page visitors by providing visual cues for the current page. Replace the home1.gif with the image called home.gif. Configure the home.gif as an image link to the index.htm page. Select the "Home" text and add a hyperlink to the index.htm file. (*Hint:* To add and modify hyperlinks, use the Property inspector. If Dreamweaver adds a border to your image hyperlink, use the Property inspector and set the border to 0.)

Next, delete the hyperlinks to the cabins.htm page. Select the cabins.gif. Use the Property inspector and delete the characters in the Link text box. Select the text "Cabins" in the text navigation bar, and delete the hyperlink in a similar manner. Finally, replace the cabins.gif with cabins1.gif to provide a visual cue in the navigation bar. Your page should look similar to the sample Cabins page in Figure 49. Save your page. Test the page in a browser. (*Hint:* F12).

So far, you've used the technique to save a web page file with a new name to increase productivity and you've practiced formatting text, creating hyperlinks, and using lists with Dreamweaver. The tutorial continues as you create the Reservations page and gain experience using tables in Dreamweaver.

Using Tables in Dreamweaver

Using a Table on the Reservations Page

Use the Save As technique to create the foundation for the reservations.htm page. Display the cabins.htm file in the Document window. Save the file as reservations.htm. The Document window now displays the reservations.htm file.

View the sample Reservations page in Figure 50. The logo and footer portions are similar to the other pages on the site. The middle portion—the content—is different. Notice how the content seems to be in two columns; it is actually a table with no border (border="0"). Let's get to work on the page.

Change the title of the page to "MooseWood Cabins :: Reservations". Delete the text in the middle portion of the web page, leaving just the logo, graphic navigation bar, text navigation bar, and footer information.

You will use Dreamweaver to create a table on the page. Place your cursor on a blank line under the graphic navigation. There are two ways to add a table to a web page using Dreamweaver. The method shown in Figure 88 is to use the Menu bar and select Insert, Table. Another method shown in Figure 89 is to use the Insert bar. Select the Tables tab, and click on the Insert Table button.

Figure 88 *Using the Menu bar to insert a table*

Figure 89 *Using the Insert Bar to insert a table*

Whichever technique you use, the Insert Table dialog box shown in Figure 90 will display. This dialog box configures table properties, including the number of rows and columns, border, and width. Set the properties so that the table has no border, one row, and two columns. The table should use 75% of the browser's width. When you are ready, click OK. Your page should look similar to Figure 91.

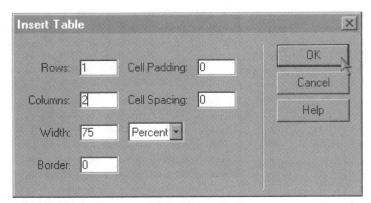

Figure 90 *The Insert Table dialog box*

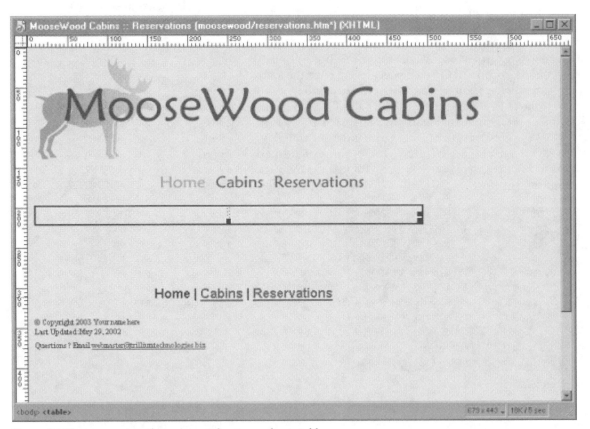

Figure 91 *The reservations.htm page with a two-column table*

The heavy lines mean the table currently is selected. The dotted line separates the columns. If you click in the table, the heavy lines will change to dotted lines and you can add text or other content to your page.

Type the following text in the left column of the table. Press the Enter Key or Shift and Enter keys where it seems appropriate.

"Cabin Rates:
$1000 per week,
Discounts for multiple week rentals

1 week minimum stay
6 people maximum
Call (218) 555-5555 or e-mail
sparky@moosewoodcabins.com
MooseWood Cabins
4000 County Rd 137
Moose Lake, Minnesota 55767
(218) 555-5555"

Type the following text in the right column of the table. Press the Enter Key or Shift and Enter keys where it seems appropriate.

"Located 1/2 mile east of I-35 at the Moose Lake exit #214. Take Moose Lake exit to County Rd 137.
Follow signs"

Your page should look similar to the one shown in Figure 92. You will notice that it still needs some work.

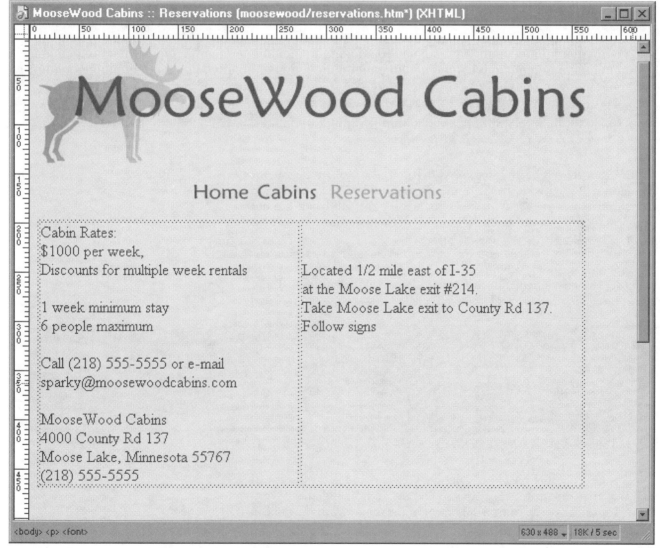

Figure 92 *The reservations.htm page with text entered in the table*

Format the text by changing the font to Arial. Bold the text where appropriate. Create an e-mail link for "sparky@moosewoodcabins.com". (*Hint:* Refer to earlier sections of this tutorial if you get stuck.)

Now let's concentrate on formatting the table and table cells. Select the table by using one of the following methods:

- Place your cursor on the border of the table and click to place heavy lines around the table and select it.
- Place your cursor anywhere inside the table. Use the Menu bar and select Modify, Table, Select Table.
- Place your cursor anywhere inside the table. Click on the **<table>** tag in the Tag Selector (Figure 93) in the bottom of the Document window to select the table.

Figure 93 *Using the Tag Selector*

- Right-click on the table to display a context-sensitive menu. Choose Table, Select Table.

Whichever method you chose, the table should now be selected and the Property inspector should look similar to Figure 94.

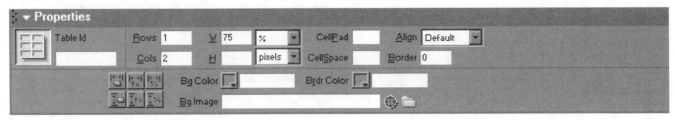

Figure 94 *Using the Property inspector to configure a table*

Notice that the Property inspector is dynamic—it looks different for each object it is used with. In the display in figure 94, the most common table tag attributes are ready to be configured. If the following are not already configured, set the width (W) to 556 pixels (the MooseWood logo is 556 pixels wide) and set the border to 0.

Dreamweaver also allows you to configure each table cell separately. Many options, including alignment, row span and column span, width, and border can be configured. Click in one of the table cells and the Property inspector should look similar to Figure 95.

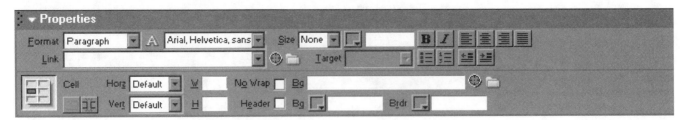

Figure 95 *Using the Property inspector to examine the properties of a table cell (<td>)*

Notice the properties specific to cells that are displayed in the lower half of the Property inspector. Modify this so that the vertical alignment (Vert) is set to Top. Change the vertical alignment of the other cell in the table in the same manner.

Now add the exterior.jpg image to the page. Drag it to the left of the *L* in "Located" at the top of the second column. Press the Enter key to move the text down to the next line. Your page should look similar to the one in Figure 96.

Cabin Rates:
$1000 per week,
Discounts for multiple week rentals

1 week minimum stay
6 people maximum

Call (218) 555-5555 e-mail
sparky@moosewoodcabins.com

MooseWood Cabins
4000 County Rd 137
Moose Lake, Minnesota 55767
(218) 555-5555

Located 1/2 mile east of I-35 at the Moose Lake exit #214. Take Moose Lake exit to County Rd 137. Follow signs

Figure 96 *The reservations.htm page with the exterior.jpg image*

Next, you will modify the navigation hyperlinks on the page. Replace the cabins1.gif with cabins.gif and create an image link to cabin.htm. Select the "Cabins" text and add a hyperlink to the cabins.htm file. Since this is the Reservations page, there is no need to link to it. Remove the hyperlink from reservations.gif. Replace the reservations.gif with reservations1.gif. Remove the hyperlink from the "Reservations" text. (*Hint:* Use the Property inspector to configure the hyperlinks. If Dreamweaver adds a border to your image hyperlink, use the Property inspector and set the border to 0.) Save your reservations.htm page.

Congratulations, you've created your first Dreamweaver site—using text formatting, images, hyperlinks, a list, and a table! Preview your web pages in a browser (shortcut key is F12) and test linking back and forth between them. If any of your links don't work or your images are broken, display the web page in the Document window and verify that your file and image names are correct. Modify, save, and retest the pages if necessary. The next section will give you more practice using tables in Dreamweaver.

Exploring Tables in Dreamweaver

Dreamweaver offers many ways to configure the appearance of tables on a web page. You can change the width of the cells and of the table visually by placing your mouse over the dotted line. When the arrow cursor appears (shown in Figure 97), you can modify the width or length of the object by dragging your cursor.

Cabin Rates:
$1000 per week,
Discounts for multiple week rentals

1 week minimum stay
6 people maximum

Call or e-mail
sparky@moosewoodcabins.com

MooseWood Cabins
4000 County Rd 137
Moose Lake, Minnesota 55767
(218) 555-5555

Located 1/2 mile east of I-35 at the Moose Lake exit #214. Take Moose Lake exit to County Rd 137. Follow signs

Figure 97 *Drag the arrow cursor to change the size of the table columns.*

Another method to configure a table is to select Modify, Table from the
Menu bar to display the Table Menu, shown in Figure 98.

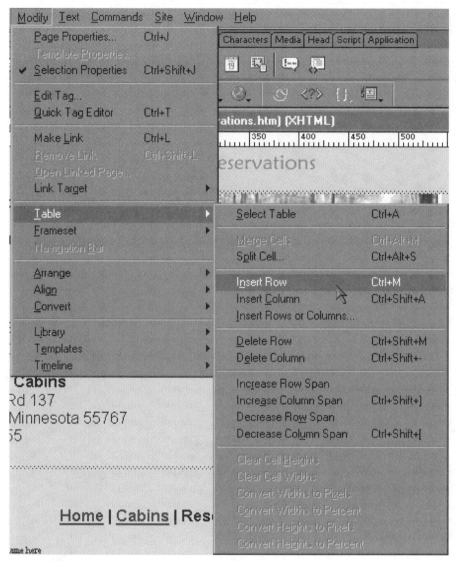

Figure 98 *The Table Menu offers many options.*

Some of the options are listed here:
- Select a table
- Merge table cells from multiple rows or columns
- Split table cells into multiple rows or columns
- Insert rows and columns
- Delete rows and columns
- Increase row span
- Increase column span
- Decrease row span
- Decrease column span
- Clear cell widths and heights
- Convert between pixels and percentages

The Table menu and the Property inspector give you great flexibility in configuring a table without ever having to write any XHTML. The next part of this tutorial will have you experiment with these tools by modifying the table on the reservations.htm page. When you are finished, your page should look similar to the new Reservations sample page in Figure 99.

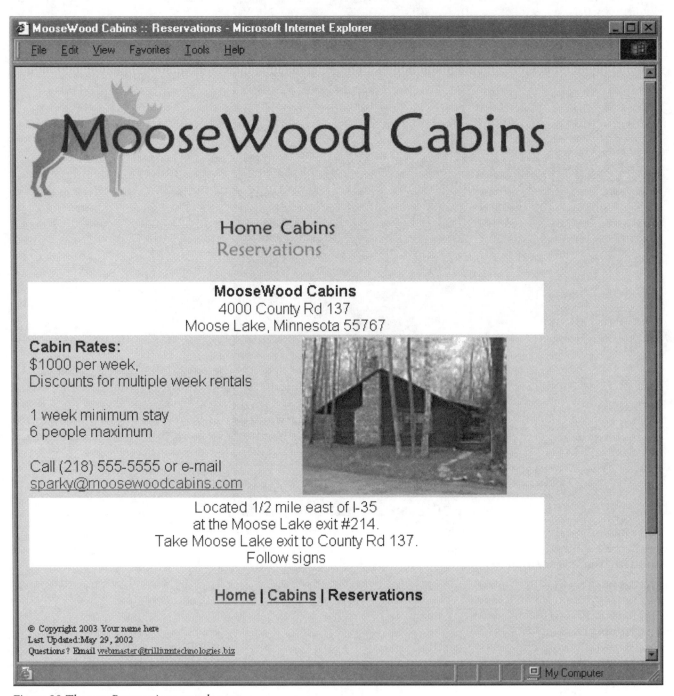

Figure 99 *The new Reservations sample page*

Notice that the address information is in its own row above the Cabin Rates and exterior.jpg. This row only has one column (cell) and has a white background. There are some differences in text formatting and cell spacing as well. Also notice that the directions are placed in their own row at the bottom of the table. This row also has one column (cell) and a white background.

Let's get started. Open the moosewood site in Dreamweaver (if it is not already open) and display the reservations.htm file in the Document window. Place your cursor in the first (the left-most) cell in the table. To add a row to the table, use the Menu bar and select Modify, Table, Insert Row (see Figure 98). This adds a row above the current top row.

Your table now has a blank row with two columns. According to our sample, the first row should only have one column. Select the two cells in the first row to highlight them. Now use the Menu bar and select Modify, Table, Merge Cells. The first row of the table now contains a single cell as shown in Figure 100.

Cabin Rates:
$1000 per week,
Discounts for multiple week rentals

1 week minimum stay
6 people maximum

Call or e-mail
sparky@moosewoodcabins.com

MooseWood Cabins
4000 County Rd 137
Moose Lake, Minnesota 55767
(218) 555-5555

Located 1/2 mile east of I-35
at the Moose Lake exit #214.
Take Moose Lake exit to County
Rd 137.
Follow signs

Figure 100 *The cells in the top row have been merged.*

Let's move the address information to the first row. Highlight the text to select it, then select Edit, Cut. Place your cursor in the first row and select Edit, Paste. Your page should look similar to the example in Figure 101.

MooseWood Cabins
4000 County Rd 137
Moose Lake, Minnesota 55767

Cabin Rates:
$1000 per week,
Discounts for multiple week rentals

1 week minimum stay
6 people maximum

Call or e-mail
sparky@moosewoodcabins.com

(218) 555-5555

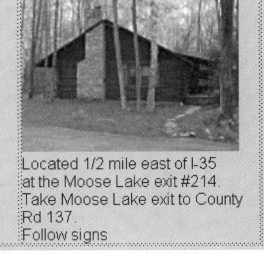

Located 1/2 mile east of I-35
at the Moose Lake exit #214.
Take Moose Lake exit to County
Rd 137.
Follow signs

Figure 101 *The address information has been moved to the top row*

Add a row to the bottom of the table. Place the cursor anywhere in the second row. Use the Menu bar and select Modify, Table, Insert Rows or Columns, as shown in Figure 102.

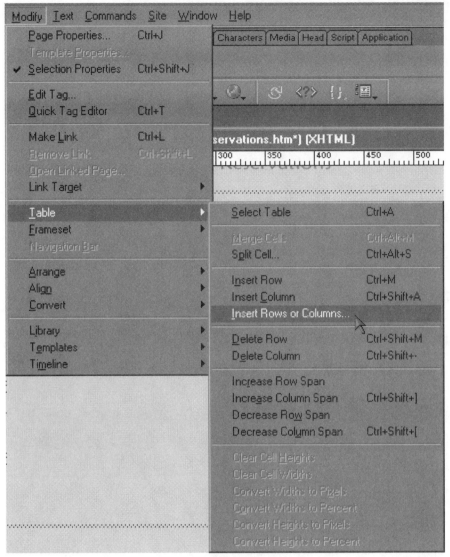

Figure 102 *To add a row below the current row, choose Insert Rows or Columns instead of Insert Row.*

The Insert Rows or Columns dialog box will display. See Figure 103 and insert one row below the selection. Click OK. Merge the two cells in this row.

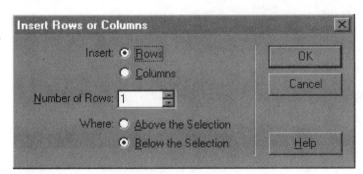

Figure 103 *The Insert Rows or Columns dialog box*

Continue to modify the page. Delete the phone number near the bottom of the first column in the second row. Move the directions down to the bottom row. Select the Table and use the Property inspector to set the cell padding (CellPad) and cell spacing (CellSpace) to 5. When needed, select a table cell and use the Property inspector to modify cell properties such as the background color (shown in Figure 104), horizontal alignment and vertical alignment.

Figure 104 *Setting the background color in the Property inspector*

Resize the cells so that there are not any large empty spaces in the middle of the table. When you are finished, save the page, view it in a browser (F12), and compare it to the sample in Figure 99. If needed, modify your page, save, and test again.

This section introduced you to some of the many table configuration options provided by Dreamweaver. The next section discusses using a table to format an entire web page.

Using a Table to Format an Entire Page

As you know, web pages are often formatted by using a table and placing all the page content within that table. In this section you will experiment with this concept by creating a new version of the Home page that is always centered in the web browser so it will look pleasing even if very high screen resolutions are used. View the sample page in Figure 105.

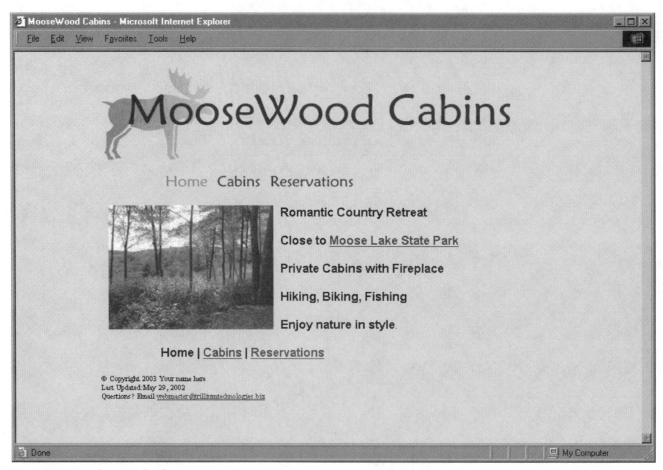

Figure 105 *Sample newindex.htm*

Let's get started and create a new version of the Home page of your moosewood site—called newindex.htm. Open index.htm in the Document window. Use the Menu bar and choose File, Save As to save a copy of the file as newindex.htm.

Place your cursor at the top of the page before the logo.gif. Insert a table (Insert, Table on the Menu bar). A sample Insert Table dialog box is shown in Figure 106. The table should be configured with one row, one column, 75% width, and 0 border. Click OK.

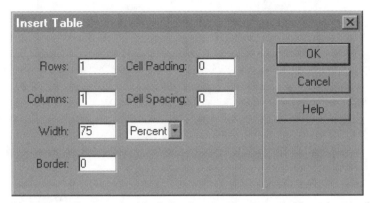

Figure 106 *The Insert Table dialog box configuring a table to format the entire page*

The next task is to center align the table. Select the table and use the Property inspector. Set the Align property to center.

Now highlight all the page content and move it to the table. (*Hint:* Either highlight and drag with your mouse or highlight and select Edit, Cut, Edit, Paste. You will find it easier to select and highlight if you start at the bottom of the page with the text and highlight upward than if you try to begin with the logo image and highlight downward.) Your newindex.htm page content should be contained in the table. If you view the XHMTL (click on the Code view button on the Document toolbar), the beginning of your page will look similar to Figure 107. Save the newindex.htm page.

```
MooseWood Cabins (moosewood/newindex.htm) (XHTML)
1  <?xml version="1.0" encoding="iso-8859-1"?>
2  <!DOCTYPE html PUBLIC "-//W3C//DTD XHTML 1.0 Transitional//EN" "http://www.w3.org
3  <html xmlns="http://www.w3.org/1999/xhtml">
4  <head>
5  <title>MooseWood Cabins</title>
6  <meta http-equiv="Content-Type" content="text/html; charset=iso-8859-1" />
7  </head>
8
9  <body bgcolor="#E8E9CF">
10 <table width="75%" border="0" align="center">
11   <tr>
12     <td><p><img src="media/logo.gif" alt="MooseWood Cabins Logo" width="556" heig
13       <blockquote>
```

Figure 107 *Code view displays the XHTML generated by Dreamweaver*

Preview your page in a browser (F12). Experiment with resizing the browser window and changing the resolution on your monitor—your page will still look good! When you are ready, return to Dreamweaver and close your pages.

Summary

This tutorial has shown you how to use Dreamweaver to insert images and hyperlinks, lists, and tables. A quick guide to common Dreamweaver tasks is shown in Table 2.

Table 2 *Dreamweaver Quick Guide*

Task	Initial Steps
New Dreamweaver Site	Use Windows Explorer (or the operating system) to create a folder for the site. Using the Site panel, select Site, New Site.
The following tasks should be done within a Dreamweaver Site.	
New page	In the Menu bar, select File, New OR in the Site panel, select File, New File.
All tasks below should be done with a web page displayed in the Document window.	
Change page properties	Select Modify, Page Properties from the Menu bar.
Format text	Highlight text and use the Property inspector.
Add a copyright symbol	Use the Insert bar Character tab and select the copyright symbol or select Insert, Special Characters from the Menu bar.
To add an image	Copy the image file to your site (use Windows Explorer or FTP). Then select Insert, Image from the Menu bar OR open the Assets panel, select the Images button, Refresh button, and drag the image to your page.
Add a hyperlink	Highlight the text or image to be the hyperlink. Modify the Link text box in the Property inspector.
Create a list	Type the text. Press the Enter key after each line. Highlight the text. Click the Ordered List button or Unordered List button in the Property inspector.
Create a table	Place the cursor on the web page where the table should be located. Use the Menu bar and select Insert, Table, then choose options, click OK.

You should not expect to be a Dreamweaver guru after completing only two tutorials. The best way to get comfortable with Dreamweaver (or any software application) is to practice with it and to use it. Try offering your web development services to friends, family members, and/or coworkers. You will benefit by having a real client to deal with. The other party will benefit from a new site. It's a win-win situation.

You have completed Macromedia Dreamweaver Tutorial 2!

This tutorial explores some of the features of Macromedia Dreamweaver MX, including:

- Using the Tracing Image feature
- Using Layout View
- Creating Flash text and buttons
- Using a form
- Using code validation and accessibility testing
- Publishing a Dreamweaver Site

Using a Tracing Image

Often web developers work with graphic designers. The graphic designer may use a graphic application such as Adobe Photoshop or Macromedia Fireworks to create an image of a new web page. Dreamweaver has a feature called Tracing Image that allows you to use this image in the Document window as a guide for your page layout and design. It is important to note that a Tracing Image is used only during development and is does not produce the page background. The Tracing Image feature allows web developers and graphic designers to easily communicate—visually. It allows a web developer to create a page layout that uses tables without worrying about rows and columns. Dreamweaver converts your Layout view into a standard XHTML table.

An example of a page layout image a graphic designer might create is shown in Figure 108. We will define a new Dreamweaver site called circlesoft and use this as the tracing image for the Home page.

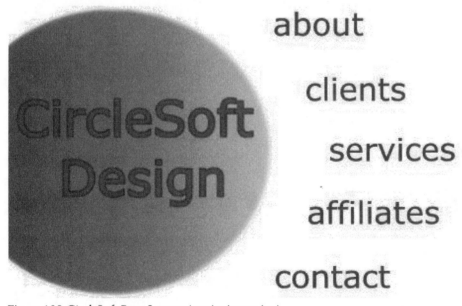

Figure 108 *CircleSoft Page Layout (tracingimage.jpg)*

Define the CircleSoft Site

Launch Dreamweaver and define a new site named circlesoft in a folder called circlesoft on your floppy or zip drive. (*Hint:* First use Windows Explorer or the Operating System to create the folder, then select Site, New Site in the Site panel.) Add a web page file called index.htm to the site. (*Hint:* File, New File in the Site panel.) Display the index.htm file in the Document window. Give the page the title of "CircleSoft Design" and save.

Add the Images to the CircleSoft Site

The images used in this tutorial can be found on the student disk in the Tutorials folder. Copy the tracingimage.jpg (Figure 108) and sitelogo.gif (Figure 109) files and save them to your floppy drive in the circlesoft folder.

Figure 109 *sitelogo.gif*

Open the Assets panel and view the images (*Hint:* F11 to open the Assets panel, click on the Images Button, Click Refresh.) Your Assets panel should be similar to Figure 110.

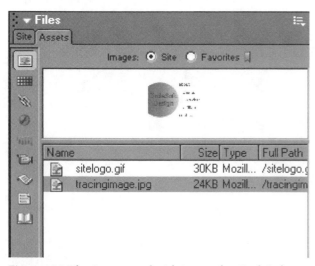

Figure 110 *The Assets panel with images for CircleSoft*

Apply the Tracing Image

Display your index.htm page in the Document window. Display the Page Properties dialog box by selecting Modify, Page Properties from the Menu bar. Find the Tracing Image text box shown in Figure 111.

Figure 111 *The Tracing Image text box on the Page Properties dialog box*

This is located in the lower third of the dialog box. Click the Browse button and select tracingimage.jpg. Click Select. Next, find the Image Transparency slider on the Page Properties dialog box, shown in Figure 112.

Figure 112 *The Image Transparency slider on the Page Properties dialog box*

Set the Image Transparency value to about 50%. Click OK. Your Document window with index.htm should now look similar to the sample in Figure 113. Save index.htm.

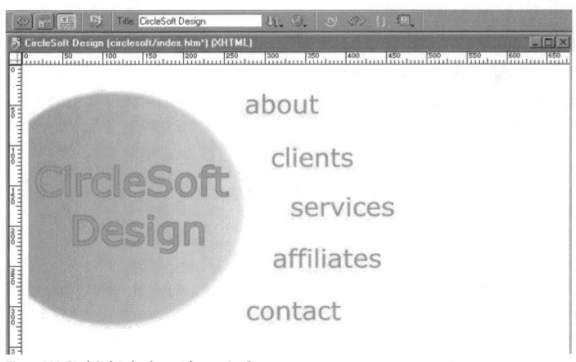

Figure 113 *CircleSoft index.htm with a tracing Image*

Remember that the tracing image will show *only* in the Document window. It is not a page background. It will not appear in a browser. The purpose of the tracing image is to help the web developer create a page based on an example created in a graphic application (usually by a graphic designer). In the next section, you will use the Layout view to design the page.

Using Layout View

Layout view is a feature of Dreamweaver that lets you visually format a page with tables. You insert "Layout Tables" and "Layout Cells" on the page. When you're ready, Dreamweaver will automatically create the standard table for you. Let's try this with the CircleSoft Home page, index.htm. It should be displayed in the Document window.

The Insert bar Layout tab lets you toggle between Standard view (normal Design view) and Layout view. Layout tables and layout cells are also configured with this area. Click the Layout View button shown in Figure 114.

Figure 114 *The Layout View button is used to change to Layout view.*

You might see the Getting Started in Layout View message box appear. It describes the Layout table and Layout cell Icons. Click OK.

Next, take a moment to notice the two new buttons available to you in the Insert bar's Layout tab (see Figure 115)—the Draw Layout Cell button (Figure 116) and Draw Layout Table button (see Figure 117).

Figure 115 *Since Layout view has been selected, the Draw Layout Table and Draw Layout Cell buttons are visible.*

The Draw Layout Cell button (Figure 116) is used to draw table cells on the page or inside a layout table.

Figure 116 *Draw Layout Cell button*

You can click inside the cell to insert content and click the cell border to move or resize the cell. If you add a layout cell to an area of the page that is not contained in a layout table, Dreamweaver will automatically create a layout table around the layout cell. The Draw Layout Table button (Figure 117) is used to draw a table on the page or in another layout table.

Figure 117 *Draw Layout Table Button*

Layout view does not need to be used with a tracing image. However, by combining the two features you can easily design a web page based on a graphic. Let's get started.

Display the index.htm file in the Document window. Use the Insert bar, select the Layout tab, and click on the Draw Layout Cell button. Move the mouse and draw a rectangle loosely around the logo area. Your page should look similar to the sample in Figure 118.

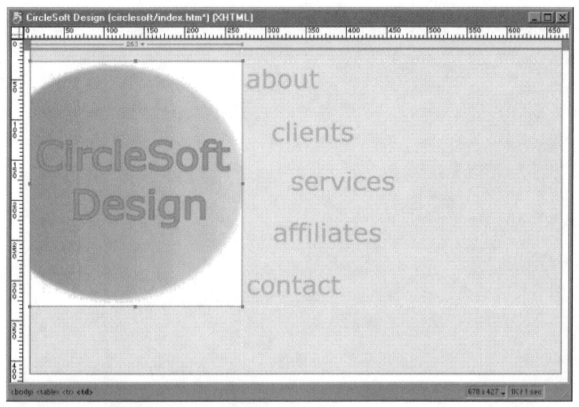

Figure 118 *A layout cell is placed around the logo area.*

The blue rectangle is the layout cell. The green rectangle is the layout table that Dreamweaver created.

Remember that the tracing image will not show in a browser. You need to add the logo image to the page. Place the sitelogo.gif image in the layout cell that you just created. (*Hint:* Select Insert, Image from the Menu bar. Drag the image from the Assets panel.) Your page should now look similar to the sample in Figure 119.

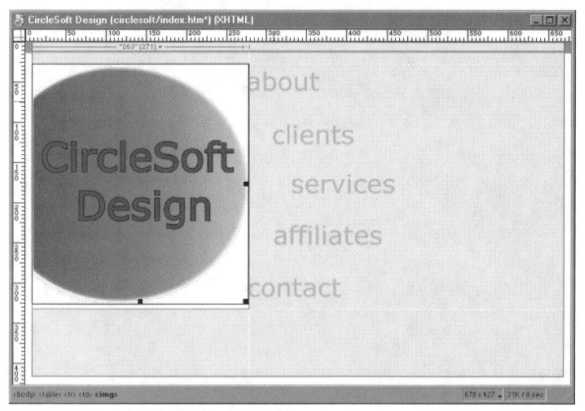

Figure 119 *The image sitelogo.gif has been added to the page.*

If you need to resize the layout cell, click on the cell border and drag until it is the desired size. Also, remember that Edit, Undo is available on the Menu bar. When you are ready, save index.htm.

Next, you will add separate layout cells for the "about", "clients", "services", "affiliates", and "contact" text. Let's start with the "about" text. Click on the Layout Cell button on the Layout tab of the Insert bar and draw a rectangle in the area of the "about" text in the tracing image. Type "about" in the layout cell. Your page should look similar to the screen shot in Figure 120.

Figure 120 *Adding text to the page*

Use the Property inspector to configure the text. Choose Arial or Verdana font, size 6. Don't worry about lining up the text exactly, just try to create a look and feel similar to the tracing image. Your page should now look similar to the screen shot in Figure 121.

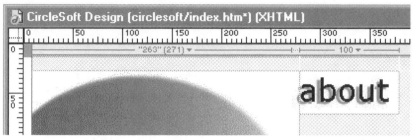

Figure 121 *The text has been formatted and follows the look and feel of the tracing image.*

Can you share some tips about layout tables?

- Layout cells *cannot* overlap.
- Layout tables *cannot* overlap.
- Layout cells do not have to be contiguous or share edges.
- The width of the layout cells is shown (in green) above the page content.

Create layout cells for the "clients", "services", "affiliates", and "contact" text using the same technique. When you are finished, compare your page to the sample in Figure 122. It doesn't have to match exactly, but it should be similar. Working with tracing images and layout tables takes practice. For this tutorial, your text does not have to exactly match the location of the text on the tracing image. However, it should match it as closely as you can. Save index.htm.

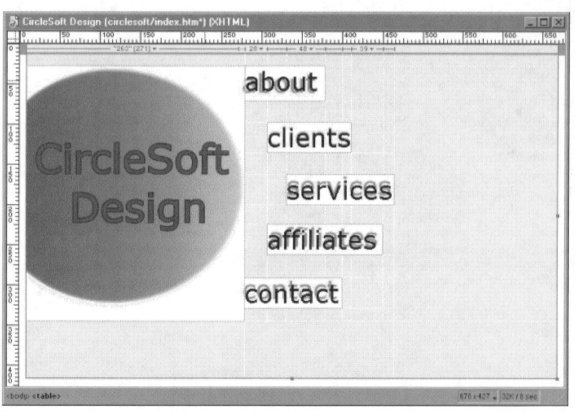

Figure 122 *A layout cell was created for each text area.*

Switching to Standard View

Now, here's the best part—you can see both graphically and in Code view the standard table code that Dreamweaver created for you. Click the Standard View button on the Insert bar Layout tab shown in Figure 123.

Figure 123 *The Standard View button*

Dreamweaver now displays the Standard view of your page. A sample is shown in Figure 124.

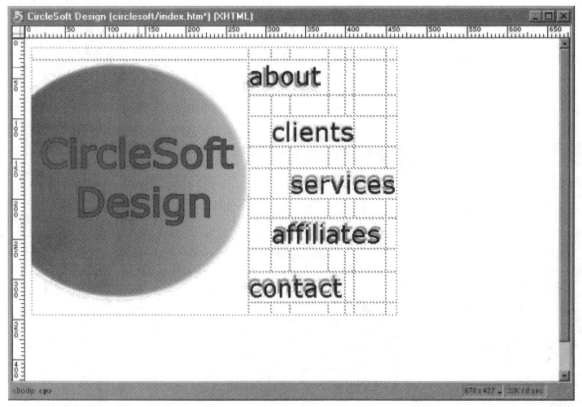

Figure 124 *The dotted lines in the Standard view indicate the table that Dreamweaver generated.*

Display the Code view (F10 is a shortcut) to examine the code. Aren't you glad you didn't have to code that table by hand?

Testing the Page

Save your page and test it in a browser (F12). Your index.htm page should look similar to the sample in Figure 125.

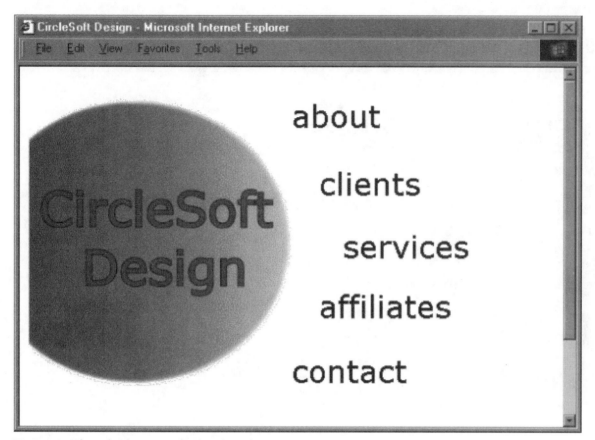

Figure 125 *The index.htm page displayed in a browser*

If you'd like the table to be flush with the margin, modify the page properties (*Hint:* Select Modify, Page Properties from the Menu bar.) and set the Left Margin to 0. Save and test your page again. A sample is shown in Figure 126.

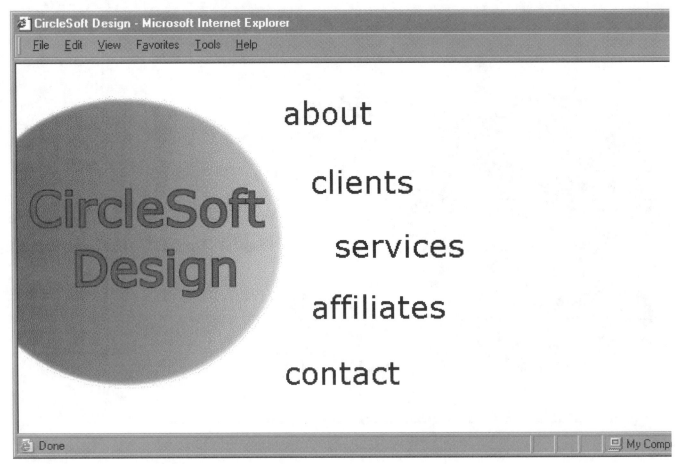

Figure 126 *The index.htm page with left margin set to 0*

Of course, if this was the actual Home page of the site, you would next create hyperlinks with the "about", "clients", "services", "affiliates", and "contact" text.

Let's recap what this section discussed. By using the tracing image, you were able to design a web page based directly on an image created by a graphic designer (or other member of your web team). Switching to Layout view allowed you to be flexible as you created layout cells and placed the items around on the page. Finally, switching to Standard view showed you the complex table that Dreamweaver automatically created for you.

The next section introduces one of the interesting aspects of Dreamweaver MX—you can create Flash text and Flash buttons right in the Dreamweaver application, without using Flash itself.

Using Flash Effects in Dreamweaver MX

According to Macromedia, over 90% of web browsers have the Flash plug-in installed. This is a very large base of users and probably includes the target audience for your site. Dreamweaver MX allows you to point and click your way to selected Flash text effects and Flash buttons. The Flash text effects and Flash buttons are saved as .swf files in your site.

The Flash text and Flash buttons in Dreamweaver provide an easy means to add some interactivity to your web pages, but there are limitations. You can only create the text effects currently offered by Dreamweaver, such as mouseovers and links. An experienced Flash designer using Macromedia Flash is still needed to create special and/or original Flash effects.

Create Flash Text

You will be surprised at how easy it is to add Flash text to your web page. Use the CircleSoft index.htm page as a working example in this tutorial. Launch Dreamweaver, open the circlesoft site, and display the index.htm page in the Document window.

You will replace the "about" text with Flash text. Highlight the "about" text and delete it. Leave the cursor in the table cell—you will add Flash text to this cell.

One way to add Flash text to a page is to use the Insert bar Media tab. Flash text and Flash buttons can also be added from the Menu bar. Use the Menu bar and select Insert, Interactive Images, Flash Text as shown in Figure 127.

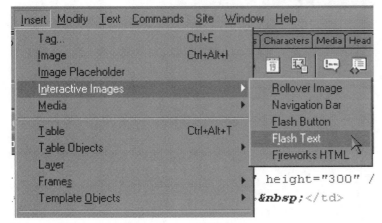

Figure 127 *Using the Menu bar to add Flash text*

The Insert Flash Text dialog box as shown in Figure 128 will display.

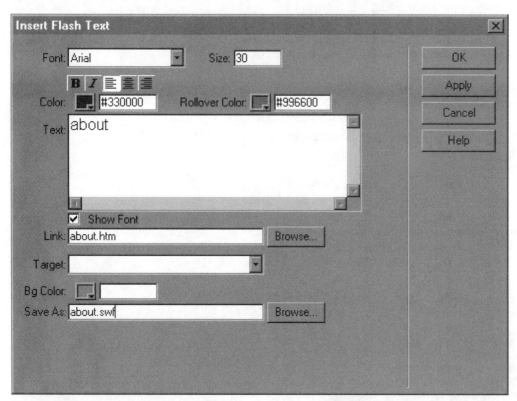

Figure 128 *The Insert Flash Text dialog box*

Configure your display to be similar to the one shown in Figure 128. Choose Arial (or other sans-serif font), a dark brown Color (text color), and a light brown Rollover Color. Type "about" in the Text area, "about.htm" in the Link text box, and "about.swf" in the Save As text box. Click OK. The Flash area on your page will look similar to Figure 129. You can resize the Flash text by dragging the edges. Save index.htm.

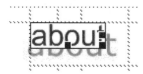

Figure 129 *The "about" Flash button*

Test your page in a browser (F12). A sample page is shown in Figure 130.

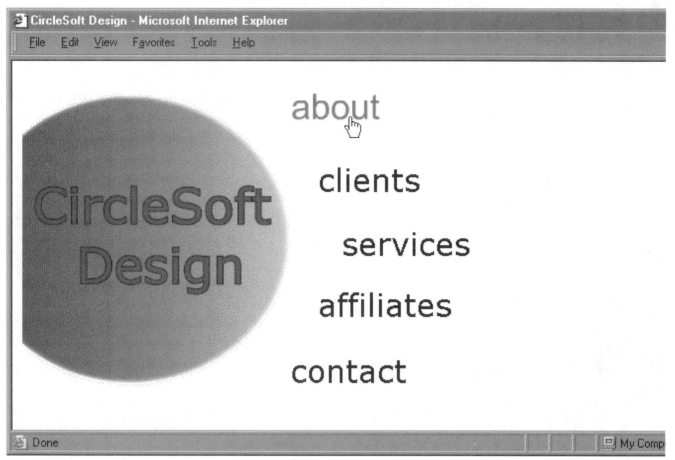

Figure 130 *The index.htm page with the Flash text in action*

Mouseover the "about" to see the text color change. The cursor should also change to the hand symbol, indicating a hyperlink. If you created an about.htm page in your site, the hyperlink would work.

Of course, if this were a page for an actual client you would create similar Flash text for the rest of the text on the page. Go ahead and do that if you'd like the practice.

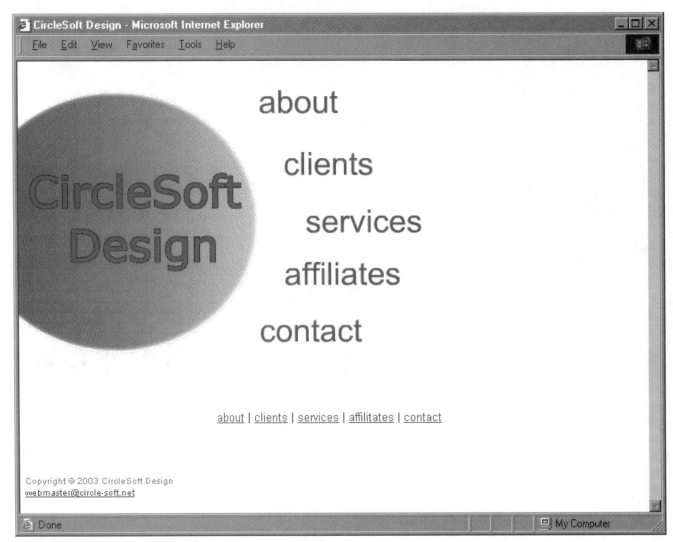

Even though the Flash Player works with a limited number of assistive technologies such as screen readers, it is a good idea to include plain text links across the bottom of a web page that uses Flash for its main navigation. See Figure 131 for a revised version of the page with a page footer containing text navigation links.

Figure 131 *The index.htm page with text links for accessibility*

Create Flash Buttons

You will also be surprised at how easy it is to add Flash Buttons to your web page. The CircleSoft index.htm page will be used as a working example in this tutorial.

Launch Dreamweaver, open the circlesoft site, and display the index.htm page in the Document window. You will replace the "contact" text with a Flash button. Highlight the "contact" text and delete it. Leave the cursor in the table cell—you will add a Flash button to this cell.

Use the Menu bar and select Insert, Interactive Images, Flash Button to display the Insert Flash Button dialog box shown in Figure 132.

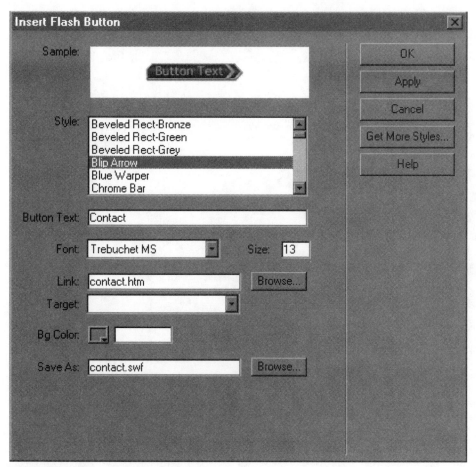

Figure 132 *The Insert Flash Button dialog box*

Configure your display to be similar to the one shown in Figure 132. Your installation of Dreamweaver may have different button styles. Feel free to choose a button style other than Blip Arrow. Type "contact" in the Button Text text box. Choose Trebuchet MS, Arial, or other sans-serif font, and leave the font size as the default for the button style that you chose. Type "contact.htm" in the Link text box and "contact.swf" in the Save As text box. Click OK. The Flash button area on your page will look similar to the one shown in Figure 133. You can resize the Flash button by dragging the edges. Save index.htm.

Figure 133 *The "contact" Flash button*

How can I get more Flash button styles?

If your computer is connected to the Internet, click on the Get More Styles button in the Insert Flash Button dialog box. The Macromedia Exchange web page will display. You can select and download a variety of Extensions to Dreamweaver, including Flash media such as Flash buttons. Have fun exploring!

Test your page in a browser (F12). A sample page is shown in Figure 134.

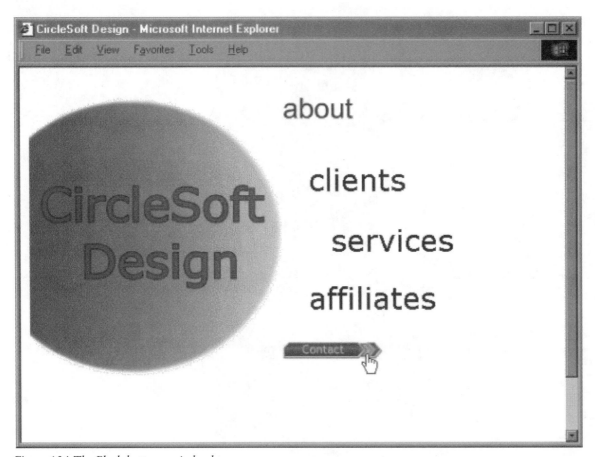

Figure 134 *The Flash button on index.htm*

Mouseover the "contact" Flash button to see the effect. The cursor should also change to the hand symbol, indicating a hyperlink. If you created a contact.htm page in your site, the hyperlink would work.

Of course, if this were a page for an actual client you would create similar Flash buttons for the rest of the text on the page. You would also create a text navigation bar (see Figure 131) that would display near the bottom of the page to provide for accessibility.

Using a Form in Dreamweaver

Forms are used for many purposes all over the Web—placing an order, creating a guestbook entry, sending a page or a news story to a friend, or joining a mailing list are just a few uses of forms. It is important to remember that there are two components to using a form:

- The web page user interface
- The server-side processing, called CGI for Common Gateway Interface, which works with the form data and sends e-mail, writes to a text file, updates a database, or performs some other type of processing on the server

In this section of the tutorial you will create the contact.htm page for the circlesoft site. The contact.htm page will contain a form. Let's get started.

Create the Contact Page

Launch Dreamweaver, open the circlesoft site, and add a new page called contact.htm. (*Hint:* Select File, New File in the Site panel.) Add content to the contact.htm page as follows:

1. Configure the page title to be "Contact CircleSoft".
2. Type "CircleSoft Design" and use the Property inspector to configure it as a Heading 1 with Arial font and dark brown color.
3. Create a text navigation bar under the "Circlesoft Design" heading. Use Table 3 as a guide.

Table 3

Text	Hyperlink Reference
Home	index.htm
About	about.htm
Clients	clients.htm
Services	services.htm
Affiliates	affilitates.htm
Contact	No link—this is the contact page

To quickly create text links in Dreamweaver, click in the Document window at the position where you want the link to appear, then use the Insert bar, Common tab, Hyperlink Button to open the Hyperlink dialog box, shown in Figure 135.

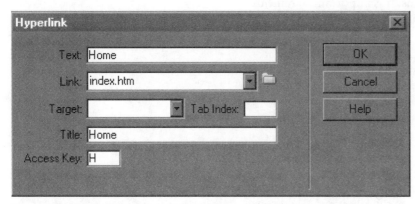

Figure 135 *Use the Hyperlink dialog box to quickly create text links.*

Configure the information needed for each link and click OK. Use the Property inspector and indicate Arial font for the links. When you have created all the text links, your page should be similar to the sample in Figure 136. Now that the basic page is created, you are ready to add the form.

Figure 136 *The text links have been added to the contact.htm page.*

Add the Form to the Contact Page

There are several ways to add a form and its objects (elements) to a web page using Dreamweaver. One method is to select Insert, Form from the Menu bar to place a form on the page. Then select Insert, Form, Form Objects to select the individual form elements. A screen shot is shown in Figure 137.

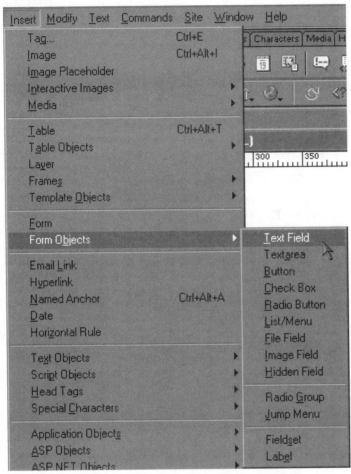

Figure 137 *Using the Menu bar to add a text field (text box)*

Another method is to use the Insert bar. Select the Forms tab and click on the Form button to insert a form. Position the cursor on the web page document and click on the Text Field button (as shown in Figure 138) to insert a text box.

Figure 138 *Using the Insert Bar to add a text field (text box)*

The contact.htm page will contain a simple form that consists of a Name text box, an E-mail text box, a Comment text area, a Submit button, and a Reset button. See Figure 139 for an example.

Name: [   ]

E-mail: [   ]

Comment:

[   ]

| Submit | Reset |

Figure 139 *The sample form for contact.htm*

Let's use Dreamweaver to create the form! Place your cursor on a blank line under the navigation bar on the contact.htm page. Select Insert, Form from the Menu bar. Your page should look similar to the sample in Figure 140. The dotted red line indicates the form.

Figure 140 *The dotted red line indicates the Form*

Next, add the objects to the form.

- Type "Name:". Insert a text box by selecting Insert, Form Objects, Text Field from the Menu bar. Press Enter.
- Add the "E-mail:" text and text box in a similar manner. Press Enter.
- Type "Comments:" and press Shift and Enter.
- Add the comments scrolling text box by selecting Insert, Form Objects, Text Field from the Menu bar. Now use the Property inspector to configure the textarea (See Figure 141).

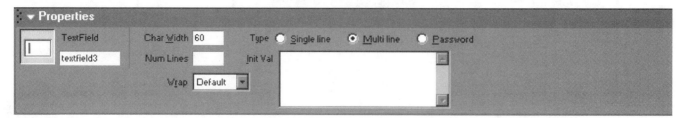

Figure 141 *Configure the scrolling text box using the Property inspector.*

- Configure the character width (Char Width) to 60 and click the Multi line radio button. Press Enter. Notice that Dreamweaver uses the TextField object to configure the text box, textarea, and password form elements.
- Add the Submit button by selecting Insert, Form Objects, Button from the Menu bar.
- Add the Reset button by selecting Insert, Form Objects, Button from the Menu bar and configuring the Property inspector to an Action of "Reset Form". Notice that Dreamweaver uses the Button object to configure both the Submit button and Reset button form elements.

Save your page and test in a browser. Your page should look similar to the example in Figure 142.

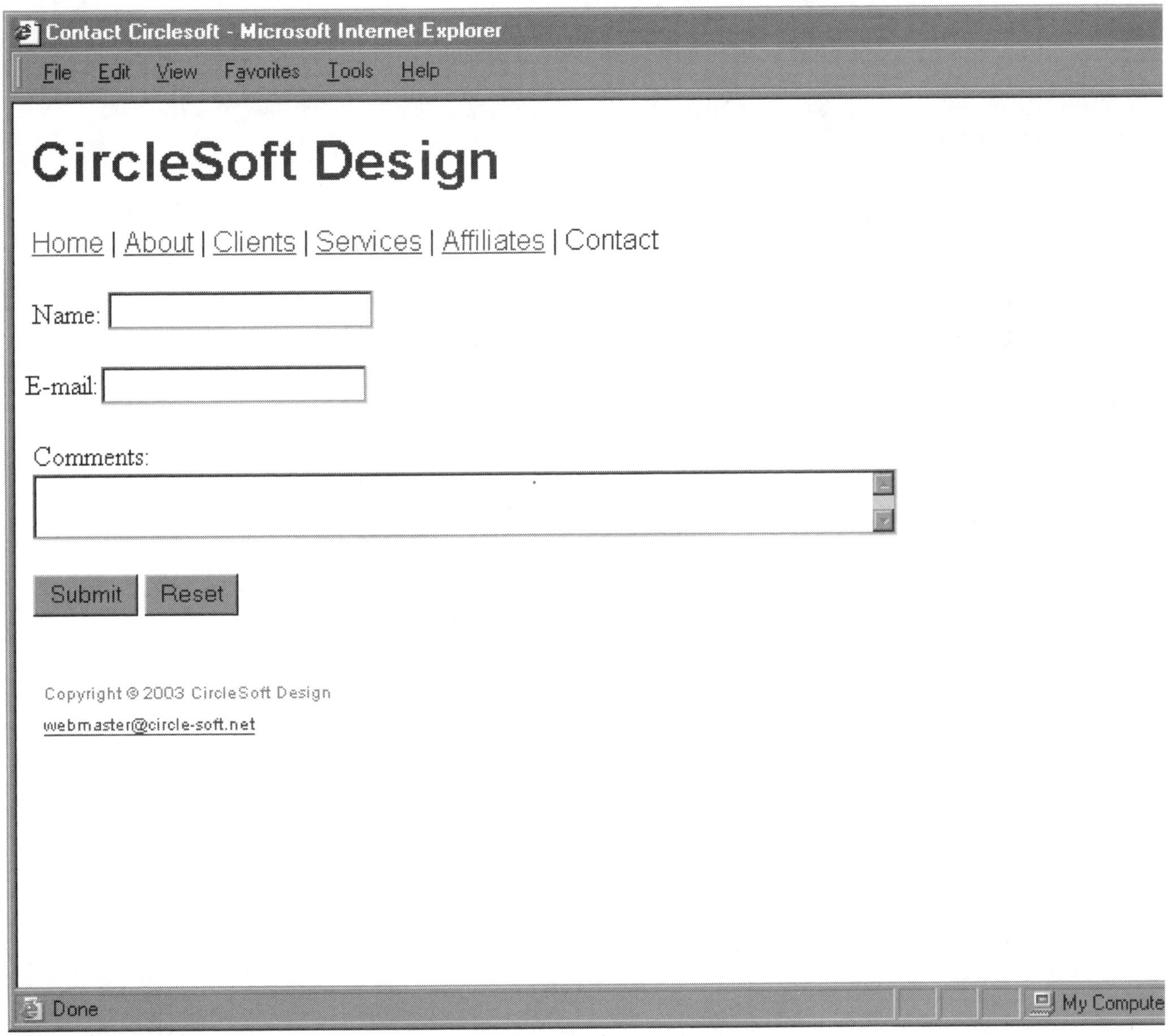

Figure 142 *The form has been added to the contact.htm page.*

As you know, in order to do its job the form needs to be connected to some type of server-side processing. The Property inspector can be used to set the action attribute of the form to the URL of a CGI (including ASP, JSP, etc.) script. The form's Property inspector is shown in Figure 143.

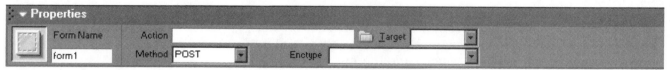

Figure 143 *The Property inspector can be used to configure server-side processing for the form.*

This section introduced you to using Dreamweaver to create a form. Be aware that most forms need to be connected to server-side processing using the action attribute on the `<form>` tag in order to do anything meaningful, such as save information in text files and databases or send form data reliably in e-mails. If you are connected to the Internet, you can use the textbook's demonstration server-side script to process the form information and display a confirmation page. To configure the form to use this script, type http://webdevfoundations.net/scripts/formdemo.asp in the Action text box on the form's Property inspector. Save the page. If you are connected to the Internet, test your page in a browser. Fill out the form and click the Submit button to invoke the server-side processing.

Now that you have created two pages in this site, let's take a look at the web page validation and accessibility checking that Dreamweaver offers.

Applying Dreamweaver Validation and Accessibility Testing

Use the Menu bar to access the Check Page option. As shown in Figure 144, Dreamweaver offers the following types of checking: Check Accessibility, Check Links, Check Target Browsers, Validate Markup (use for HTML), and Validate as XML (use for XHTML).

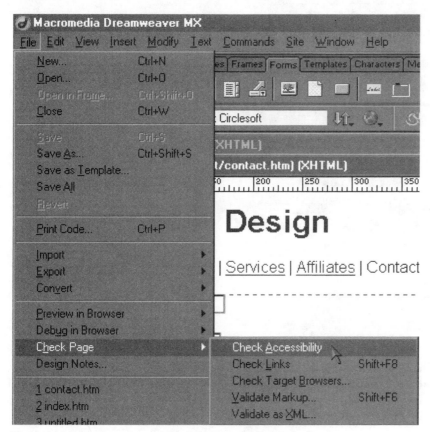

Figure 144 *Dreamweaver can check for accessibility compliance.*

"Check Accessibility" tests a page for compliance with both the Section 508 and W3C Guidelines. "Check Links" tests the internal site links and reports on any that are broken. It will also list external links for you to manually verify. "Validate as Markup" is used to validate HTML web page documents. "Validate as XML" validates web page documents coded in XHTML or XML. When this test was run on the contact.htm page, one error was reported, as shown in Figure 145. It shows the line number with a description of the problem. It seems that the **<textarea>** tag should have a rows attribute. If you add this attribute (either in Code view or with the Property inspector, the code will be considered technically correct.

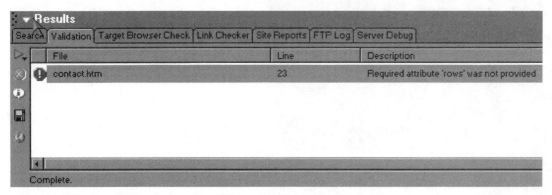

Figure 145 *The Results panel after the "Validate as XML" page check*

Now that you are becoming comfortable with both coding and testing in Dreamweaver, let's find out how to use it to publish your site.

Publishing a Dreamweaver Site

You can use an external FTP application to publish a Dreamweaver site. However, Dreamweaver also offers a built-in FTP publishing feature as part of the Site panel. This section of the tutorial explores using this feature. If you take a moment (OK, maybe a few moments) to obtain free site space, you can try out the publishing along with the tutorial.

Configure Site Preferences

Before using Dreamweaver to transfer files, you should configure a few site preferences. Select Edit, Preferences from the Menu bar. Choose the Site Category as shown in Figure 146.

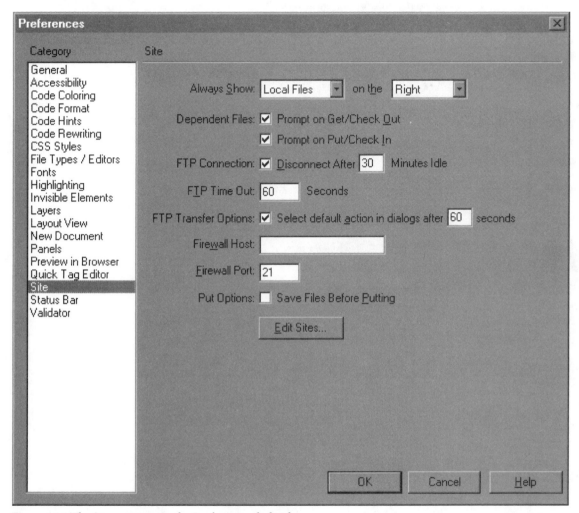

Figure 146 *The Site category in the Preferences dialog box*

If you are connecting to the Internet from behind a firewall you may need to configure the Firewall Host and the Firewall Port options. Contact your network administrator for the correct values.

There are a number of options that you may configure in the Preferences dialog box. You can change the way that the Local Files (files on your computer) are shown, whether you will be prompted for dependent files (such as images), the FTP idle time disconnect and time out-values, and whether files are saved before being uploaded.

In most cases, the default Site Preferences are workable. Click OK.

What do these FTP Terms mean?

- **GET** refers to downloading a file *from* a web server to your computer.
- **PUT** refers to uploading a file *to* a web server from your computer.
- **FTP Idle Disconnect** refers to the number of minutes that the connection will be kept open when there is no activity or file transfers.

Configure the Remote Site

Now configure the Remote Site information for the particular site you are working on. Select Site, Edit Sites from the Site panel. The Edit Sites dialog box appears and is shown in Figure 147. (Your site list is expected to be different from the list in Figure 147 because it contains the names of the Dreamweaver sites you have defined.)

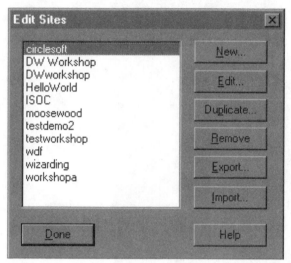

Figure 147 *Begin with the Edit Sites dialog box when you need to set up a remote site.*

Select the name of your site, such as circlesoft, and click the Edit button. The Site Definition dialog box will appear. Select the Remote Info Category. Your display should be similar to Figure 148.

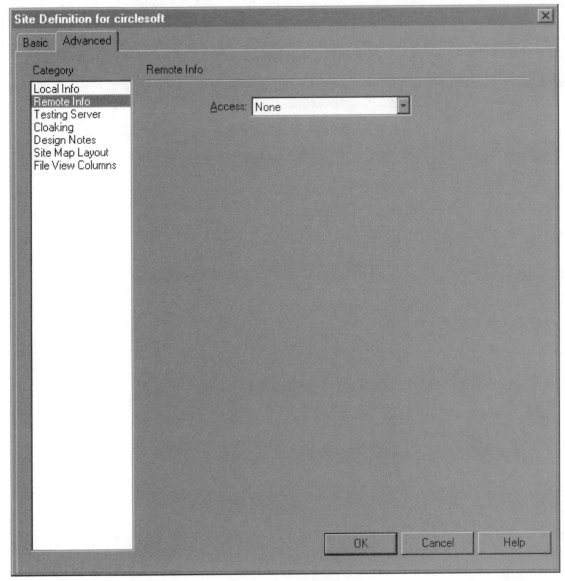

Figure 148 *The Remote Info category on the Site Definition dialog box*

Click on the list box next to "Access" and choose FTP. Your Site Definition dialog box should be now be similar to the one shown in Figure 149.

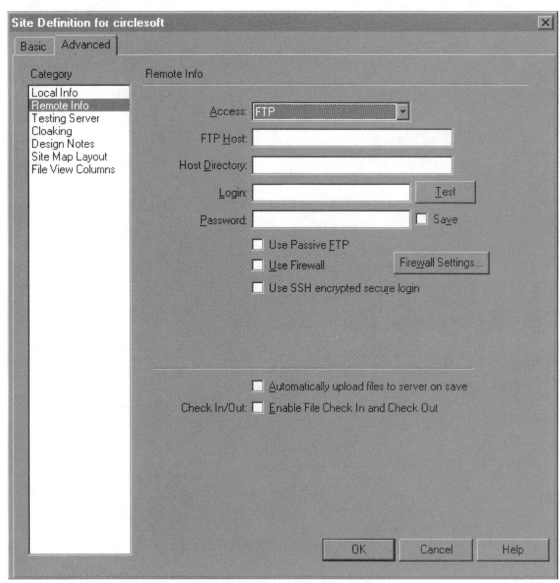

Figure 149 *FTP has been selected to access the remote site.*

Your web host provider will have given you the values that you need to enter in this dialog box. For example, the author's web site account with Free Prohosting (http://free.prohosting.com), a free web host provider, is stored on the web server named "odin.prohosting.com". The web host provider has supplied the username "cisweb" and a password value. There is no specific host directory (it is based on username). They also have indicated that they use passive FTP. A screen shot of the dialog box with that information is shown in Figure 150.

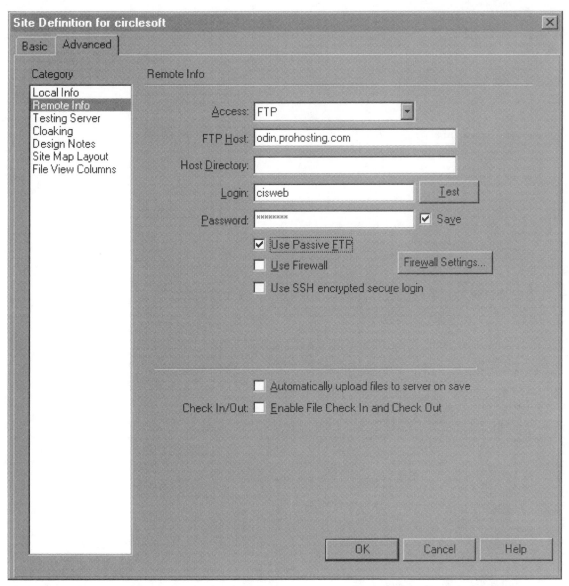

Figure 150 *Ask your web host provider for the information you need to complete this dialog box.*

Use the configuration information given to you by your web host provider and configure the Site Definition information. When you are ready, click OK and the Define Sites dialog box appears. Click Done.

Connect to the Remote Site

There are a number of ways to use Dreamweaver to connect to your remote site. One method is to select Site, Connect from the Site panel. See Figure 151.

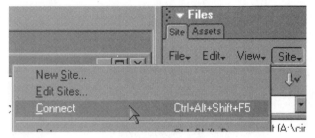

Figure 151 *Connecting to a remote site*

A message box will appear that displays the status of the connection process. Figure 152 shows one of the messages.

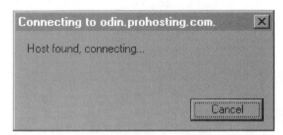

Figure 152 *Dreamweaver will display messages as it attempts to connect.*

If there is a problem with the connection, an error message will appear (perhaps you typed your username or password incorrectly, or need to change the Passive Mode setting). If all goes well, you will see a brief "connecting" message and the Site panel will display the Remote view—the files on the web server. To see both the Remote view and the Local view (the files on your computer) at the same time, click the Expand/Collapse button on the right-hand side of the Site panel Toolbar (see Figure 153).

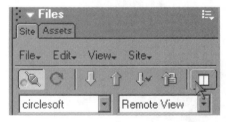

Figure 153 *The cursor is pointing to the Expand/Collapse button.*

When you click the Expand/Collapse button, the Site panel will fill the Dreamweaver workspace as shown in Figure 154. The Site panel will display the Remote Site (web server) on the left side and the Local Files (your computer) on the right side.

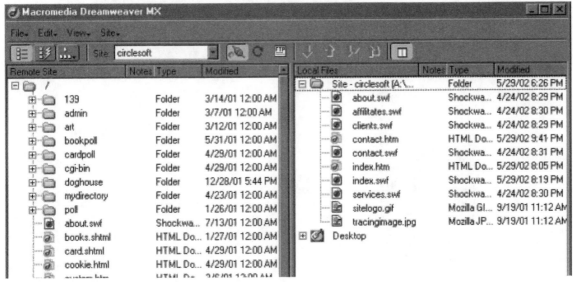

Figure 154 *The Site panel fills the Dreamweaver workspace*

Don't worry if your screen does not show the same folders as shown in Figure 154. This Remote Site has been used before and it contains a number of folders and files. Your Remote Site will probably just contain an index.htm or index.html file if you recently acquired your free web site space.

Use Folders to Organize the Remote Site

Since the Remote Site is used for a number of purposes (just as your free web site space can be used for a number of assignments or projects), it would be a good idea to create a separate folder for the circlesoft site. (*Note:* You do not have to create folders on your web site space. You may transfer to the root directory of a site without creating folders. The folder is used here to organize the web site space.)

Figure 155 *The Remote Site Folder icon*

To create a special folder for the "circlesoft" site on the Remote Site, click on the Remote Site folder icon (shown in Figure 155) and select File, New Folder from the Site panel. Name the folder circlesoft.

Figure 156 *The Refresh button*

Click the Refresh Button (Figure 156) on the Site panel Toolbar to refresh the display. As shown in Figure 157 the circlesoft folder is now on the Remote Site.

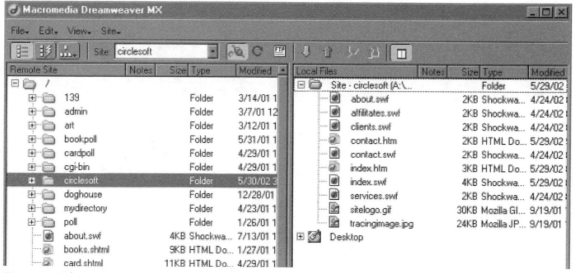

Figure 157 *The Remote Site now contains the circlesoft folder.*

Upload to the Remote Site

There are a number of ways to upload or put the files from the Local Folder to the Remote Site. One method is to select a file and drag it to the appropriate folder on the Remote Site. Transferring a file to the Remote Site does not delete it from the Local Folder. Another method to transfer files is to first select and highlight the files to be sent in the Site window Local Folder. Next, use the Site panel and select Site, Put. You also could have clicked the "Put" button (shaped like an Up arrow) in the Site panel toolbar.

Figure 158 shows the Site Window after the circlesoft files have been transferred.

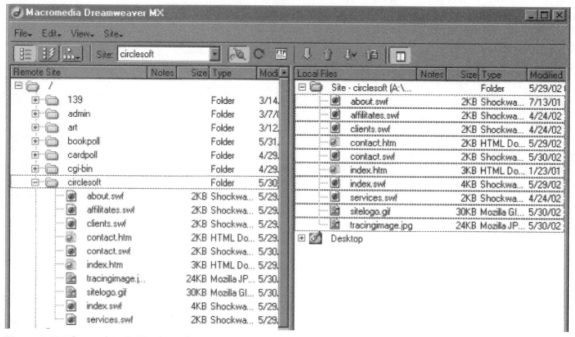

Figure 158 *The circlesoft files have been transferred to the Remote Site.*

When you are done transferring files, disconnect from the Remote Site by selecting Site, Disconnect from the Site panel. Remember to return the Dreamweaver workspace to normal by clicking on the Expand/Collapse button (see Figure 153).

Test the Remote Site in a Browser

The next step would be to use a web browser and test your site. Your web host provider supplies the URL for your site. The URL for this free site happens to be http://odin.prohosting.com/cisweb, and the files were placed in the circlesoft folder. So, to test the site, use http://odin.prohosting.com/cisweb/circlesoft as the URL, as shown in Figure 159.

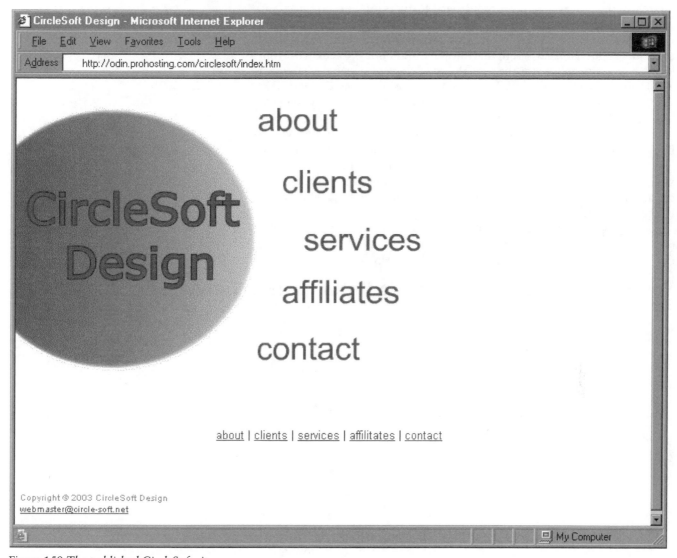

Figure 159 *The published CircleSoft site*

Files can be downloaded from web servers in a manner similar to the one shown for the upload. Connect to the server and drag the files from the Remote Site to the Local Folder. Remember, GET means download and PUT means upload.

This completes the whirlwind tour of transferring files using Dreamweaver. The purpose of this section was to get you started and to enable you to publish your sites using Dreamweaver. There are other options that you can experiment with on your own as you become more comfortable with the application.

Summary

This tutorial provided a brief introduction to some special features of Dreamweaver MX—tracing images, layout view, Flash text, Flash buttons, code validation and accessibility testing, and publishing. There is so much more to learn about Dreamweaver. These tutorials have only scratched the surface of the productivity features of this popular web authoring tool.

Options to continue your study of Dreamweaver include college and continuing education classes, online tutorials, and books. Check with your local community college for the availability of classes on web development and Dreamweaver. If online (free) tutorials are more your style, try searching the Web for "online tutorial" or "Dreamweaver tutorial"—you might be surprised at the resources that you find. There are many books that provide information and practice exercises with web authoring tools. Visit a bookstore (online or brick-and-mortar) and take a look at what's there. A good guide to purchasing a technical book is to quickly scan a topic that you already know and scan a topic that you don't know. If you like the way the author treats both topics and find it easy to read, the book will probably be helpful to you.

One thing that is certain is that the Web never stops changing. The sooner you get used to learning on your own, the better. If you are a web development professional, count on continuous learning.

You have completed Macromedia Dreamweaver Tutorial 3!

Index